Make It Nice

Make It Nice

DORINDA MEDLEY

GALLERY BOOKS

NEW YORK LONDON TORONTO SYDNEY NEW DELHI

Names and identifying details of some individuals have been changed.

G

Gallery Books
An Imprint of Simon & Schuster, Inc.
1230 Avenue of the Americas
New York, NY 10020

First Gallery Books hardcover edition August 2021

GALLERY BOOKS and colophon are registered trademarks of Simon & Schuster, Inc.

For information about special discounts for bulk purchases, please contact Simon & Schuster Special Sales at 1-866-506-1949 or business@simonandschuster.com.

The Simon & Schuster Speakers Bureau can bring authors to your live event. For more information or to book an event, contact the Simon & Schuster Speakers Bureau at 1-866-248-3049 or visit our website at www.simonspeakers.com.

Interior design by Jaime Putorti

Manufactured in the United States of America

10 9 8 7 6 5 4 3 2 1

Library of Congress Cataloging-in-Publication Data
Names: Medley, Dorinda, author.
Title: Make it nice / Dorinda Medley.
Description: First Gallery Books hardcover edition. | New York : Gallery
   Books, 2021. |
Identifiers: LCCN 2021016838 (print) | LCCN 2021016839 (ebook) | ISBN
   9781982168322 (hardcover) | ISBN 9781982168339 (paperback) | ISBN
   9781982168346 (ebook)
Subjects: LCSH: Medley, Dorinda. | Real housewives of New York City
   (Television program) | Television personalities—United States—Biography. |
   Women television personalities—United States—Biography.
Classification: LCC PN1992.4.M456 A3 (print) | LCC PN1992.4.M456 (ebook)
   | DDC 791.45/028092 [B]—dc23
LC record available at https://lccn.loc.gov/2021016838
LC ebook record available at https://lccn.loc.gov/2021016839

ISBN 978-1-9821-6832-2
ISBN 978-1-9821-6834-6 (ebook)

I dedicate this book to the two most important
women in my life:
my mother, Diane Cinkala,
and my daughter, Hannah Lynch.

At the end of the day, we can endure much more than we think we can.

—FRIDA KAHLO

CONTENTS

Make It Nice

INTRODUCTION

If I could go back in time and give some advice to the young girl from Great Barrington, Massachusetts, who climbed trees so that she could carve out a place of her own and think, away from her two brothers and sister and the surveillance of her mother, I would tell her to stop worrying about the destination and trust in the journey. To not be afraid of falling short or taking a misstep and to embrace life as it happens. I would tell her that a person is shaped as much by their failures as they are by their successes.

Yes—that girl is me. When I was young, I would look out from the treetops and imagine what the world looked like beyond the bubble of my home. I had no idea what was out there. All I knew was that I had to see it.

It's funny that, right now, I am writing a book about my life in the same Great Barrington, a town I so desperately wanted to venture beyond. I spent my early life devising ways to leave this small town in the Berkshires. And then, after many years of adulting life, I tried my hardest to figure out how to return home.

As a young girl I used to idolize a house on a hill that was a mile from our home. It seemed so far out of reach. Well, somehow, many years later, I now find myself owning this home. What had once seemed out of reach was now mine. Sometimes, when I look out the window, I think, *How the hell did I get here?*

I've spent the last forty years in many places: Great Barrington, New York, Hong Kong, Australia, Paris, Vienna, Germany, London. During this time, I've created successful businesses and taken pride in my work, be it as a Liz Claiborne associate, an aerobics instructor, a cashmere designer, a real estate agent, a mother, or a housewife (for both my own family and later my Bravo family). I have had great loves in my life that didn't turn out the way I expected. I never imagined I would end up a divorcée or a widow when I got married, but now I can say that I'm glad for both of these experiences. My first husband and I didn't make it, but together we raised an incredible daughter with the help of our new life partners. Ours is a family of stepparents and stepchildren whom we never referred to as "step." What says it all is that my first husband was one of only a few people who were at my second husband's bedside when he died.

I'm going to quote my mother a lot in this book, because she is one of my greatest influences. She once told me that the most beautiful wines in the world are made from the grapes that struggle the most. Those grapes have thicker skin, and they might look a little more beat-up than the pretty grapes, but inside they have an incredibly rich juice. They're perfectly imperfect, and that's what makes them so delicious.

For the majority of my life I was fearful of showing the imperfect sides of myself, of falling short of the "ideal," of being a "bad" mother, wife, daughter, or friend. I believed perfection was the definition of success and that if I could be the best mother, the best wife, and the best daughter I would feel fulfilled. The problem with this, however, is that I left the best me out of that equation. I let myself be defined by other people's opinions of me and found myself not knowing what I liked, wanted, or desired.

Before I decided to join Bravo's *Real Housewives of New York City*, I'm not sure I fully knew who I was beyond the roles I played for other people. I knew myself as Dorinda Cinkala, the daughter of John and Diane Cinkala. I knew myself as Dorinda Lynch, the wife of Ralph Lynch and the mother to Hannah Lynch. And I certainly knew myself as Mrs. Medley, the powerhouse wife of Dr. Richard Medley.

But who was Dorinda?

I was determined to find out. I was done wasting my time trying to please other people. I accepted that I was perfectly imperfect and I stopped needing everyone to like me. And the most amazing thing happened. I finally started to feel free.

Anyone who has seen me on *The Real Housewives* probably knows that shiny façades do nothing for me. I want to know what's really going on behind that façade. I gravitate toward people who show up authentically as themselves because that's how I like to show up now—as myself.

The decision to become a more authentic version of myself didn't happen overnight. Old habits run deep. About a year after Richard died, I was asked to attend a lunch for the Council on Foreign Relations. When I got the invite I thought, *Of course I need to go. This is important; this is prestigious; this is what I should be doing as a widow of Richard Medley.*

But I was miserable. For the first time I thought, *This is not me anymore. This is not where I want to be.* Don't get me wrong, it was a gorgeous event, but it just wasn't me anymore. So I left. I made the decision that in the future I would no longer do things that made me miserable.

It was right around this time, just as I was settling into my skin in a new way, that I was approached to be a castmate on *The Real Housewives of New York City.* What better thing to do with my realness than be on reality television?

It was strange that I became a Housewife right after I lost my husband. But in another way, it was perfect because it signaled independence at the exact moment I was stepping into my new resolve to live more selfishly. Being on *The Housewives* was the first time in my life that I did something that was just for me. I wasn't Dorinda Cinkala anymore, or Dorinda Lynch, or Dorinda Medley. I was just Dorinda.

At fifty-six, I finally feel I am living a life I have ownership over, a life that is the culmination of years of experiences, choices, and lessons, both good and bad. I understand myself in a much healthier and happier way. I've set myself up financially, I take care of myself physically and spiritually, and I'm surrounded by loving, smart, motivated, and kind people. I'm happy to be my age. Sure, it might be nice to wear a midriff and do cartwheels, but I've enjoyed the grace and the insight that have come with aging. I am my perfectly imperfect self. What all of this amounts to is a life filled with the capacity to explore, enjoy, entertain, and grow. I guess you could say I've made it nice!

And now I want to tell you how you might do the same. Making it nice is not just about the outside stuff. It's about making it through. It's about getting knocked down and getting up again. It's about surviving.

Life is like hosting a dinner. It takes a lot of preparation. It doesn't just happen. This book will be like me inviting you over hours before the party starts to see all the work that goes into creating the final product. I'm going to tell you how I've become a woman who's learned to accept herself, flaws and all. And I'm going to tell you the real story of how I got here—the good, the bad, and the ugly.

If you're struggling, my hope is that after reading this you might have some new ideas about how to take ownership of your life, express yourself as an individual, lean into your sense of independence and self-worth, and embrace your journey, even if it seems imperfect. Starting is the hardest part of any journey. So, on that note, let's get started!

***

Life is like reading a book. You think you know how it's going to end, but the final chapters often surprise you.

Chapter One

ON PAUSE

In August of 2020, I was gearing up to start the next season of filming for *The Real Housewives of New York City*, just as I'd been doing for the previous six years. My life in those six years had taken on a new rhythm. For four months, while we filmed the show, I ate, drank, and lived *The Housewives* twenty-four hours a day. And then, for the rest of the year, I was making plans for the upcoming season. Participating in the show was a bit like the Olympics or opening night at the opera. You have to prepare yourself mentally for months before filming. You watch reruns. You think about what you want to showcase. You strategize. You arrange parties. You brainstorm places that would be fun to go as a group. And then, before you know it, it's show time again.

If you aren't on a reality show, you're probably not thinking about how to play a dramatic game of chess with your friends, but when you're on reality television that's exactly what you're thinking. You're like a military general in high heels, strategizing and attacking, perpetually reevaluating your situation and thinking about how to win. And in the world of reality television, the definition of "winning" is very different. If you're too nice, your castmates will perceive you as being vulnerable. If you're too mean, the world will.

If you think the show is scripted, it's not. You walk in never knowing what's going to happen. You paste on a poker face of confidence, ready for the prospect that at any moment you could be blindsided. And you've got one shot to get it right, because there are no "redos" or "reshoots." For all your planning, the strategy usually goes down the drain in the heat of the moment—which can result in what they call reality TV gold. Sometimes you come up with a zinger out of nowhere. I wasn't thinking about how "not well, bitch" would become a phrase I could put on a mug when I first said it, for example. Sometimes you say something you never intended to say or even meant when you said it, but you have to go with it or else you'll be eaten alive. Housewives are like sharks. They can smell blood in the water, so you better be sure not to bleed.

Even when you apologize, there is often no space for it, no way for it to land securely in the way you might want. Sure, I can say I'm sorry and mean it when I say so, but that doesn't mean that I know how it will be received or how it will be portrayed on the show. You can't stop the boulder once it's started rolling downhill. You just have to let it land where it lands and hope you don't get squashed in the process.

The goal of a reality TV show, and of any TV show, is to entertain, and a lot of the entertainment on *The Housewives* stems from conflict and interactions. Because, let's face it, would you honestly watch the show if it were a documentary about a bunch of women sitting around at a dinner table being nice to one another? Of course not. That would not be very interesting. Reality television is empathetic escapism. For an hour, you get to live someone else's life. Life is messy and complicated, and without the dirty details it wouldn't be very relatable. When you film a reality TV show, you're not looking for thoughtful responses from your audience; you're looking for big reactions—the types of reactions that make you spit your beverage out of your mouth and jump to your feet.

Ironically, for a reality TV show, filming the show enters you into a different type of reality. It has some semblance of the real world but in other aspects is totally removed. The process has a fun way of making your real life fade into the distance. There is no longer enough time for the people you love; there's no longer any room for the things that make you *you*. For a brief period, you enter a parallel universe where the camera crew, the production staff, and your castmates become your whole world.

The sudden stop that comes after filming is totally disorienting. It's a bit like vertigo—the feeling of movement and spinning goes on even when you are standing in place. And the anxiety, don't get me started on the anxiety! You've stated your case, and now the jury is out.

The other thing is that if it doesn't happen during the filming season, then it kind of doesn't exist. A lot of times, what you don't see is just as important as what you do. Scenes you thought were great sometimes get cut, and scenes you wish you could forget become the main focus. There is one characteristic that binds all the Housewives to one another, and that's bravery. For a second, imagine what it would be like to have someone documenting everything you do and say, knowing that millions of people are going to judge you for it. You have to be fearless or you simply won't make it.

After filming, I do my best to leave my *Housewives* drama behind. I go back to my life as Dorinda Medley and as Hannah's mom. I go on long walks with friends; I watch funny Instagram videos; I think about getting a dog and then decide against it; I leave the city and go back to Blue Stone Manor—my house in the Berkshires—and spend time with my parents. I'm not Dorinda the New York Housewife anymore. I'm Hannah's mother, John and Diane Cinkala's daughter, and a friend to my many friends. I'm me again.

You don't *really* forget about the show after you stop filming the season, but you do kind of put it in the back of your mind. There is no denying that in the quiet moments at the end of the day, when I was doing the dishes, or washing my face, or worst of all just lying in bed watching *Law & Order*, thoughts about the show would creep into my head. I'd find myself watching what we filmed play out on my bedroom ceiling, and I'd start thinking about what I could have done better. After filming, the questions you consider over and over are, *Who will I be when this new season airs? What will my parents think? What will my daughter think? What will the world think?*

While the process can be stressful at times, the positive definitely outweighs the negative overall. Filming is fun and you laugh your ass off more often than you cry your eyes out. Taking the plunge into the outrageous is liberating because you are able to lean into the most exaggerated version of yourself. In the world of the Housewives, being uninhibited is a good thing and social niceties fall out of the window—which is great for me because I hate small talk. There's a lot of joy that comes with being on reality television. It's fun and exciting and I always felt lucky to be a part of it. It takes a village to raise a child, as they say, and it takes an even bigger one to make a season of *The Real Housewives of New York City*. It's an intense experience for everyone involved, and the crew and producers become your lifeline. They're the only people who understand exactly what you're going through. It's like a family or a sorority.

So, back to 2020. As I was gearing up to film Season 13, everything that had happened in Season 12 was on my mind. Honestly, watching Season 12 unfold was *a lot*. To some degree, I had expected this, because the reality was that I'd had a rough year. I broke my rib. My father got sick. My house flooded. All the remnants of my life with Richard were floating in our basement. As I watched the dump trucks take it all away, I felt like I was right back to where I had been ten years before. It wasn't just that he was gone. It was that *our life was gone*. It was like a big aquatic monster had broken into my house. We had to put major holes in the walls and use extraction heaters to dry out the house. There were cracks in the plaster and paint peeling from the walls. Our house, meaning mine and Richard's, was ruined. The last time I had renovated this house was with Richard, and for years I took comfort in being surrounded by the decisions we made—and now all of that was literally falling apart before my eyes. I had to redo the home we made together, only this time I had to do it alone. I just remember crying so hard to my mother and thinking, *I can't fall apart; I have to fix everything by the time filming starts. I have to get it done for our seasonal Berzerkshires episode.*

Instead of giving in to my sadness, I picked myself up again. I took the flood as a sign that I needed to let go of my old life, to begin anew. It was time and I knew it, but that didn't make it any less painful. I ended my relationship with my then-boyfriend, John. The hardest decisions are almost always the right decisions, and although we loved each other, I realized it just wasn't meant to be a relationship that lasted for the long term. It was wonderful for a while, and then it was meant to end. We broke up because it was time for me to move forward and I needed to do that on my own. I still care about John a lot, and he will always have a seat at my table.

I got the house done in time for the show, but when we started filming I wasn't in a great place, and that definitely came through in Season 12. Because of my brutal honesty and the fact that I'm always willing to fight, I'm often a somewhat villainous character. This season, though, it was more intense. I remember saying to a friend, "This was not my best season, but next season will be better."

And then I got the call from production.

"Hi, Dorinda, we're going to take a pause. We want you to take a year off and really enjoy your time and then we'll revisit this next year."

I was shocked. "What? I don't want to take a pause."

But they insisted. "No, no, we're going to take a pause."

I just couldn't believe it. Wasn't I a beloved character? Weren't my ratings high? Didn't I have a ton of Instagram followers? To a normal person, all this might sound unimportant, but in the land of reality television these are measures of success. In this land, numbers count. Social engagement counts. Fans count.

"I don't understand," I said. I was in tears.

The production company reiterated what they'd already told me. The conversation was going nowhere and I was too emotional to continue, so I got off the phone.

A few minutes later, Andy Cohen called. He said many warm things to me. He told me I was iconic and reminded me that it wasn't necessarily good-bye forever. It was just a pause.

I didn't understand this word. Pause? If Bravo wasn't going to extend an offer for the following season, wasn't that like being let go? Wasn't it like being fired? And if I was being fired, then why were we using the word "pause"?

As I mentioned before, I'm not into façades. I don't like sugar-coating things. I just don't understand it. If I'm wearing a white shirt and somebody tells me they love my pink shirt, what am I going to say? I'm not going to say, "Thank you." I'm going to say, "Thank you, but it's a white shirt."

"Andy, it sounds like I'm being fired," I said.

Andy insisted it was a pause, and a friendly one.

I still didn't understand what was going on, but there was no point in fighting. "Thank you for the opportunity," I said. "It's been a fantastic six years."

Honestly, I felt like a big fat loser. Being rejected is painful. And I'd never been fired from a job in my whole life. I have an excellent work ethic and I take pride in that. I believe that any job, big or small, should be treated with total respect. That's how I've treated all my jobs. When I was a waitress, I never missed a waitressing shift. Even if I was dying, I would still show up for work. In six years, I rarely missed a day of filming for *The Housewives*. I was never late. I was fully devoted to it in the same way that I fully devote myself to anything I'm doing. *The Housewives* had become an enormous part of my life, and I was heartbroken that it was ending for the moment.

I didn't ask why I'd been put on pause. I didn't want to know. To me, that part wasn't important, because it wouldn't have changed the result. The decision had already been made. But, of course, since I'm only human, I had to wonder why. Had I done something wrong? If so, what?

I knew that because it had been a hard year for me, I hadn't shown up as my best self. I also knew that I'd never been a passive character on the show. My honesty is one of my greatest strengths, so I've been told, but it also gets me into trouble sometimes. I'm not always nice in my delivery. Once in a while, I hurt people.

I don't like injustice, and when something unjust is happening around me I can't stop myself from calling it out. When I was a kid, I used to stand up for the kids at school who were being bullied. I've always spoken the truth, even when my opinion isn't popular. And that's what I did on the show.

Here's a little saying I enjoy: Believe half of what you hear and all of what you see.

For so many people, what they see is not connected to what they say. The mouth is not connected to the heart. I think this is especially true for women, because there's so much pressure to pretend. Sometimes I think my life would be easier if I were a woman who was willing to pretend. If I just went along with things and stayed quiet, people would be less angry with me. But it's not in my nature to go along with things that are just plain incorrect. I hate pretending. I find it unbearable. When there are lies in a room, I feel like the room is full of elephants. I can't ignore them. I have to speak up. What I'm trying to work on now is *how* I speak up, because I realize I can come across as abrasive at times.

I'm fully aware that I'm more abrasive when I'm drinking. During this rough year in my life, I was drinking more than I wanted to be. When I'm in a good period of my life, I drink to have fun, but when I'm in a dark place, it just makes things darker.

So, after I got fired, did I have some regrets? Yes. I also knew I couldn't have done anything differently. The past was the past, and there is no point in wallowing. I did allow myself to be upset the night I got those calls, though. I sobbed like a child and called my mom, who talked some sense into me, as she's been doing all my life. Then I invited a few friends over and drank wine and kept sobbing.

The next morning, I woke up knowing that a new chapter of my life had begun. I posted a picture of myself on Instagram with a caption about gratitude. I thanked Bravo and NBC for the opportunity and wished them success in the new season.

I felt good about my public reaction. Even though I believe in honesty, there are times when it's best to just say thank you and walk away. And I'm good at walking away. Even though I hate change, I'm able to let things go quickly and move forward.

When the news of me being put on pause went public, friends started calling me and asking, "Are you okay? What are you going to do now?"

The truth is that I'm not doing anything differently than I would have been doing otherwise. Yes, we're in a pandemic, so that sort of changes things, but otherwise, my life is the same as it's always been. Hannah asked me if I was still going to decorate for Christmas last year, even though it wouldn't be filmed, and I said, "I've been decorating for Christmas for forty years, Hannah. Of course I'm going to decorate this year!" Beneath all the changes in life are the things that never change. I'm always going to love being a part of my family. I'm always going to love decorating. I'm always going to be outspoken. I'm always going to be essentially myself. As I told Bethenny Frankel on her podcast, *The Housewives* didn't make me. I was a fully baked cake when I arrived, and I gave them a slice.

It's funny that I was a Housewife for six years, because that time span marks a pattern in my life. Every six years or so, things change in a drastic way. I lived with Hannah's father, Ralph, for six years before we separated; I was later with Richard for six years, and then with John for about another six.

Since I was raised Catholic, it's hard not to draw a parallel between the number six and the devil. Every six years, it's like the devil invites me for a little dance. At first it's horrible, but then it becomes a place to transform. Funnily enough, the devil card in tarot signifies transformation.

When major shifts happen, after I get over the initial blow I sink into a quiet, determined place, where I reconnect with my soul and my purpose. The reason I'm able to do this is that I've built myself a strong foundation. My family is a foundation for me, and so is my connection to my soul, or to something greater than myself. It's easy to get lost in the drama and hoopla of life, but in the end, none of that matters very much.

What I remember in every moment of change is that I don't need to define myself by one label. Labels aren't helpful, and I see a lot of women getting stuck on who they think they should be rather than looking ahead to who they can become. I've had many labels in my life so far. I've been a waitress, a salesperson, an aerobics instructor, a clothing designer, an expat, a mother, a wife, a hostess, and a Housewife, to name a few. I'm not any one of these labels, though. I'm just a woman moving through her life creatively.

After the shock of getting put "on pause" wore off, I realized that it wasn't a failure. It was freedom. I've never had a "pause" in my whole life. And failure isn't real anyway. It's just an opportunity to rise up again. To be honest, there's something I enjoy about getting knocked down. I do well when I have less. It gives me energy.

It makes me curious about the future. *What can I learn during this time? What are the next six years going to look like?*

Right now is a strange moment in history. The whole world is on pause, wondering what's going to happen. Of course, I have no idea what's going to happen, but I do know that no matter what the future holds, I'll always be me, Dorinda Cinkala from Great Barrington, Massachusetts.

**If you don't know yourself,
no one will be able to know you.**

Chapter Two

HOME

I was born in 1964 to an Italian mother and a Polish father. My parents met at eighteen in a very classic and romantic way. My dad saw my mom walking down the street and said, "That's a beautiful woman and I want to marry her." Within eight years, they had four children: Johnny, Dean, Dorinda, and Melinda. We're each two years apart.

Growing up, we weren't raised as individuals in the way kids are today. Let's just say there weren't *options, like children have today.* In the Cinkala household, my mother was the captain of the ship. We did what she said without questioning it. She set the tone and we followed. For example, if it was cleaning day, we cleaned. If it was yard day, we were outside. We weren't picky about our food, because there was no room to be picky. We accepted what we were given, and with gratitude. When we would go to restaurants and be given menus, we would look at them the way people normally do, but when the waiter came it was no surprise that we all got the veal cutlet Parmesan special. We didn't think to challenge it; that's just the way it was.

Recently, I saw a child literally pull down his pants and show his bum to everyone in the middle of a Starbucks—but that wasn't the horrifying thing. The horrifying thing was that when it happened the mother crouched down eye to eye with the boy and was like, "Use your words." My siblings and I never would have been this defiant—not even close. It wouldn't have even crossed our minds to enter into a negotiation over what size hot chocolate we were getting. Our family could best be described as the segments of a caterpillar with my parents at the head. When they moved we moved; it rippled through all of us.

The weird thing is that my siblings and I were all totally different to the point that people probably questioned whether we were even related when they saw us playing in our driveway.

First there was Johnny, who was nothing like the typical tormentor older brother. He was kind and encouraging—the person who brought us all together and acted as the intermediary between us and our parents. But even though he was the most responsible and organized of us all, he was also the wackiest.

When we were little and my mother would take us to the grocery store, she would make sure that we all held on to the cart because she was petrified of us getting kidnapped. Everything would be fine and well, the Cinkala unit moving smoothly through the aisles, until suddenly Johnny would take his hand off the cart and go into spaceship mode. It would start small with him putting his hands to his sides and then he would start making a quiet revving noise to indicate that the ship was preparing for liftoff. We all knew what was coming and my mother would tell him to stop, but the launch was happening whether she liked it or not. By the end of it, Johnny would be in the middle of the aisle with his hands in the air (his arms would be stiff and vibrating), rumbling and spouting off crackly throaty noises. *"Khheee-oooohh, khoo, khee-oooh."*

When he was young, my second brother, Dean, was very much a stereotypical boy. He collected baseball cards, slept in a Steelers sleeping bag, and did all the very boyish things that you would expect. He was also a real pain in the ass and spent most of his time pushing our buttons, which probably had something to do with the fact that he was just smarter than we were. Dean was also incredibly sensitive, which made him a ticking time bomb. We spent a lot of time playing board games in the basement, and after hours of Monopoly, Dean would get up and flip the board over because he hated losing. One time Johnny, who was a gentle giant, got so fed up that he dragged Dean around the pool table by his legs until he got rug burns. I think it was *because* Dean was so sensitive that he was mischievous and disruptive as a kid.

Dean grew out of his mischievous side, and his sensitivity evolved into something far more earnest. Less carefree than Johnny, Dean was serious and thoughtful, always thinking one step ahead. He was the type of kid who would give unsolicited advice that you would want to reject but couldn't because deep down you knew he was right. Dean became my protector, particularly in high school when I was most vulnerable. He didn't like the idea of me dating. He protected me fiercely from the boys and was always looking over my shoulder to make sure I didn't get into trouble. He would drive me to and from dances, dragging me out of them when I wanted to stay longer—which I *hated*. Dean's thoughtfulness was the thing that made him a good big brother. He genuinely cared and showed it by never being afraid to tell you the truth, even if it was something you didn't necessarily want to hear. It's hard to be the villain sometimes, but it's the people who aren't afraid to be the villain when it means telling the truth whom you can depend on the most.

Melinda, my sister, will always be the baby of the bunch. Unlike me, who could be a bit of a bulldozer (surprise, surprise), Melinda had a gentleness and naïveté that made her more susceptible to getting hurt. She has no guile. The fact that she was the only one of us who got sunburned when we went to Florida as teenagers is a perfect metaphor for who she is. I can still remember her sprawled out on the hood of our car with sunstroke when my mother insisted we attend a four-hour service at an Evangelical church.

When I was a teenager, the fact that we were so different used to really drive me crazy. After I got a job at the Red Lion Inn, they were so impressed with my waitressing skills that they brought my sister on. It was a nightmare. There was one dinner service where we were serving beef au jus, and were expected to bring it out on a tray in this larger-than-life way, which I loved. Well, at some point I looked back, and Melinda was not only *not* using a tray (but rather just her hands), she was also pinching the side of the gravy boat with her thumb and forefinger—with her thumb literally inside the gravy boat. Melinda doesn't have a mean bone in her body and is very intelligent. She's simply not of this universe and her priorities are not material. She's pure of heart and now runs a hospice for dogs out of her home in Sheffield, which says it all.

Melinda and I couldn't have been more different, but she was in many ways my best friend. There was a yin and yang quality to the two of us. She was my partner in crime or maybe more like my sidekick. I often took advantage of her good nature. When we got Barbie stuff and were dividing up the clothes, I would convince Melinda that the bad clothes were the best and she would just accept it without question. I don't know if it was because we were both girls or because we shared a room together growing up, but I always felt like Melinda got me in a way that others didn't.

When I was seven or eight years old, I started talking through my pointer finger, which I referred to as "Pinky," moving it up and down like a finger puppet and speaking in this raspy, nasal, creepy voice. My mother hated it. Of course she did! It was totally bizarre. If Hannah ever did the same thing to me, it would freak me out. The only person who engaged with my game wholeheartedly was Melinda, who would have full-on conversations with Pinky before we went to bed.

The last sibling I need to tell you about is me.

Dorinda is an old Italian name, and it happens to be my mom's middle name, too. My mother wouldn't allow anyone to shorten my name or give me a nickname. I remember when I went off to school she said, "Don't let anyone call you anything other than Dorinda. You are Dorinda Cinkala." There was a pride to the way she said that to me, and it was a pride that I internalized. We were proud to be Cinkalas.

Everything my siblings and I had growing up was because my parents worked for it. Although we didn't have a lot of money, we were comfortable and I never felt like we didn't have enough. It took me a long time to realize how my mom, in particular, knew how to economize. When I got to college, for example, I was exposed to a new kind of orange juice. At the buffet were these enormous containers of it. The first time I poured myself a cup and took a sip, I spit it out. It tasted like pure sugar.

And this was because my mother used to buy that canned orange juice concentrate that comes frozen in a tube, the kind you mix with water. You're supposed to mix it with two cans of water. Well, my mother would mix it with eight cans. And that watered-down tangy liquid was my conception of orange juice. When I went home, I told my mom about what I had discovered at college and asked her why she had been fooling us with orange water.

"I couldn't afford to give you orange juice every day, Dorinda," she said.

This sounded strange to me because orange juice wasn't exactly expensive, but to my mother, who was always two steps ahead, a sugary drink meant cavities, and at that time we simply couldn't afford to get our teeth filled. My mom was crazy about our teeth. She used to line us up and have us brush and floss endlessly. Good dental care was important to my mom because she wanted to make sure we had every possible advantage going out into the world as adults. My father's lifelong work as a telephone man for the New England Telephone and Telegraph Company thankfully covered those expenses. So while we didn't have a lot, it didn't matter because my parents made sure that we always had enough—and enough felt like everything to us.

And yet there was also a sense that there was something *more* waiting out in the world for us. What it was didn't matter so much as the fact that it existed. My parents never pushed my siblings and me to become anything specific, like doctors or lawyers, but they taught us to have dreams and to always be moving forward in pursuit of our goals. The journey was more important than the destination. The pride of being a Cinkala meant that you could do anything so long as you worked hard enough to achieve it. Everything I am today is because of who my parents are.

I wrote a paper about my father as a child that my mother saved in a binder called "Dorinda's Memorabilia." In this paper, I wrote: "My father is the best. I couldn't say why he is the best, but he just is and I love him so much and he loves me."

I think I had a hard time figuring out why I loved my dad so much, because he was always working. He was a telephone man by day, and by night he'd pick up extra jobs whenever he could. But just because he wasn't physically at home didn't mean I couldn't feel his presence. The fact that my dad worked so hard made him a hero to me. When he worked as a telephone operator at night, I would sneak down to the basement to call him when my mom wasn't paying attention. It was the coolest thing to me. I could pick up the phone, dial 0, and there was my father. To me, my dad wasn't just a worker. He was this giant person who literally ran the telephone lines in Great Barrington. My dad was like a king in my eyes.

On the weekends, despite being so tired, he still would do activities with us like fishing and hunting. In a small town like Great Barrington back then, gender roles were real. There were certain things that boys did with their fathers, like hunting, and certain things that girls did with their fathers, like getting an ice cream. We never subscribed to those roles. My siblings and I did everything together. My parents raised me to believe that boys and girls were equal. I wasn't freaked out by bugs, because my father would spend all night with us using mustard sauce to lure out the night crawlers so we could go fishing the next day. I picked them up and put them in coffee cans like it was nothing. We all caught our own bait and we all baited our own rods. With fishing and in all other areas of life, I was taught that if I worked hard and took the steps necessary to succeed (like collecting my own bait), then I would reap the rewards of my efforts.

Unlike my mother, my father wasn't born in Great Barrington. He is originally from Brooklyn, born to Polish immigrant parents. As a teenager, my father was singled out because of how smart he was and picked to go to Bronx Science, a high school for gifted teenagers. He got perfect grades and was on a straight track to college—until his father bought a farm in Great Barrington. My grandfather got cancer right after they moved, and this massive farm became my father's responsibility. Everything my father dreamed for himself was gone—poof—just like that. Every day my father would wake up before dawn, milk the cows, collect the chicken eggs, and then head to school, where the kids would make fun of him because he smelled like farm animals. Listening to him talk about how beloved he was by his friends at Bronx Science and how he had won all these academic rewards before he was forced to leave is always somewhat heartbreaking, but there is never any sense of resentment or tragedy in his voice. It was because of this that he made sure his children had all the opportunities that he didn't have, and I think he lives vicariously through our successes.

Now let me tell you about the most important figure in my family: my mother. My mother was and is my world.

My mom's job was to run the household with intent, like it was business. Just because my dad was bringing home the weekly paycheck didn't mean my mother wasn't working. Our house was like a business center. Every Friday my father would obediently bring home his paycheck and hand it to my mother. From those paychecks, she would give my father an *allowance* to go play his weekly poker game with his friends (which still happens to this day). Our household was a well-oiled ship—but then again, there was a natural chaos that came with having four children under the age of eight at twenty-six years old. She was completely devoted in all ways. The house was spotless, she cooked every day, and most important, she was available to us and to my father 24/7.

I had no idea until I became a mother myself how difficult it was for my mom to manage to do it all. Later, when I had Hannah, I was living in London and I had a baby nurse and a housekeeper and I found the complete and constant devotion to *one* child sometimes overwhelming. How did my mother do it? In retrospect, I see how hard it must have been. Married at nineteen, four children, responsibilities and not a lot of money to work with, and somehow she did it each and every day with the commitment of a professional athlete. My mother embodied what it meant to be a Cinkala, and like her, we were expected to work hard, to do our part, to take care of one another, and to stay constant.

If my mother was the rock that we all relied on, the rock that my mother relied on was God. I think God gave my mother the space to imagine the future and to find balance in the present. God meant that there was nothing too big to be unconquerable, because the good of God was always bigger than the bad of the moment. Looking back, I realize my mother took great refuge in religion and especially in prayer. Watching my mother pray is almost magical. It's the type of thing that makes you want to cry. Experiencing her faith is enough to make you not only believe but also take part.

As kids, we did take part, and without questioning it. Religion was a constant presence—and I mean that both literally and metaphorically. There were life-sized statues of Mary and Saint Anthony all over the house. My mom was a devout Catholic, but she was never militant about it. What religion gave us was a moral compass. It acted as a second parent that was "always watching"—which was both comforting and scary. Sure, God's teachings were about morality and spirituality—"love thy neighbor as you love thyself" was a big one—but my mother also used to tell us that the Ten Commandments would keep us out of jail, which felt like it was less about religion and more about how to stay out of trouble. I guess you could say that religion gave us a set of bumper rails for life. Like getting my period or my first training bra, religion was just a fact of life for me growing up.

In some ways, my mom has become more of a relaxed Catholic these days. Or at least she's started to question some of the stories. A few years ago, she said, "I don't know if I believe in that Noah's Ark thing anymore. It doesn't really make sense that they had two of every animal on a boat for all those days."

We were all beyond shocked when she said this. Her admitting to an affair would have been less surprising than her questioning Noah's Ark.

"Maybe it wasn't exactly as the story goes," she said. "Maybe there weren't two of every animal on the boat."

"Mom," I said, "if we're going down the controversial road here, what about Adam and Eve?"

"What about it?"

"Do you think it was real?"

"Yes, it was real, Dorinda! Don't ask me silly questions like that."

These days, I still go to church, but I go because I want to go, not because I feel that it's an obligation. For me, spirituality is not governed by Mass times and locations. It's wherever and whenever I need it. Church to me is similar to what yoga, therapy, or meditation is to other people. I find it peaceful. It allows me to quiet my mind. I love the stories and the smells, because it reminds me of childhood. It gives me time to reflect and reset and have a quiet and confidential conversation with God. It gives me the feeling that all is well. Stay steady, stay accepting, and keep going: these are the reminders of church.

The cast of important characters in my young life included not only my parents but also my grandparents. My mother's parents, Vera and Adorno Joseph Magadini, had the biggest presence because they lived a bike ride away. My grandfather was an especially influential figure, not only because he came over almost every day but also because of the way he took up space in a room. At six feet two, he was a big figure with a huge personality to match. He was loud and fun and handsome and irreverent but still totally elegant. He loved his community. He also didn't follow the rules. I remember him waking me up in the middle of the night to watch Evel Knievel on television. In my other memories, he's surrounded by food and laughing and having a great time just being alive. In a lot of ways, I am like him.

My grandfather found success in America when he opened a masonry business called A.J. Magadini and Sons. The name proved to be telling because my mother was excluded from the business, despite her devotion to my grandfather and her intelligence. Similar to my father (who had to leave Brooklyn and his education behind), my mother was offered a full scholarship to college, which was a big deal for a woman back then, but was told that there was no point in her going. My mother was no Gloria Steinem or Betty Friedan, but she was a strong feminist—even if she didn't realize it herself. And therefore, she was adamant about her daughters and sons being treated equally and having all the same opportunities—including the ones that, unfortunately, hadn't been granted to her. I decided that I was never going to allow what happened to my mother to happen to me.

I think that it was because I was most like my grandfather that I was willing to spar with him. We both had strong personalities, and I didn't fear him like the other members of my family did. I spoke up. We were very close and we spent tons of time together.

On Friday nights, we kids all stayed at our grandparents' house. We would get out of school on Friday afternoons and rush to find my grandmother at the local hairdresser, where she had a standing weekly appointment to get her hair washed. My grandmother liked a routine. A heavyset Italian woman with silver hair, she, like my mother, took her job as the woman of the house very seriously. She cleaned her house daily and buffed her linoleum floors as if the Pope would be arriving at any minute. She went through cans of Lemon Pledge like nobody's business, and she would never have thought to leave her house before all her tasks were completed and she had taken her daily bath, which included the same products every time: Dial soap, Jean Naté body powder, and Jergens lotion. She kept these products in what she referred to as the pigeonhole, which was a small nook in the hallway. She'd yell, "Kids, get my lotion in the pigeonhole!" After her bath, she would powder her face and apply lipstick. My grandmother took pride not only in who she was but also in the way she looked.

Every Friday, I'd rush to her as if I had not seen her for ages. She was warm, loving, and all the things that come to your mind when you think of the perfect grandmother. She adored her grandchildren and we adored her. She loved to tell stories and gossip about her neighbors, and we would hang on her every word. She also liked to gossip about the soap operas she watched religiously at three o'clock. We'd discuss the drama between Luke and Laura on *General Hospital* as if it were factual. I loved my grandmother so much and often still think of her and her nonstop stories and the smell of all her products.

Fridays marked the beginning of our secret life with my grandparents. We were allowed to do things with my grandparents that we were not allowed to do at home with my parents. This included eating Devil Dogs, Twinkies, Snoballs, white bread, cold cuts, Coca-Cola, and chocolate Fudgsicles and other branded ice cream, like Friendly's. We got to stay up late and watch Carol Burnett, Cher, and *Saturday Night Live*. It was magical, accessible, and abundant.

One of my responsibilities at my grandparents' house was to take the weekend donut order. On Friday nights, I would meticulously write down what each member of the family wanted and draw accompanying pictures to hand to the women at Spudnuts donuts early Saturday morning. I took this job very seriously.

Before going to Spudnuts, my grandfather and I would take a trip to the barn to feed the chickens together and collect eggs. I was always amazed, driving around in his dump truck, at how he seemed to know everyone. He was like the mayor of Great Barrington.

My grandfather expected me to become the same type of traditional woman as my mother, but I knew that that would not be the case. I already knew that one day I was going to move out of Great Barrington and be a big shot. When my grandfather and I drove past the manor in which I now live and I pointed at it and said, "I'm going to buy that house," he laughed at me. He was familiar with the house because he, along with his father, had helped build it. He was a mason worker. That was his station in life. And he didn't believe that I, as a female, could rise to a higher station. But I didn't care. I was going to show him.

My Polish grandparents on my father's side were also important influences on my early life, but we didn't see them as often because they lived in Clark, New Jersey. My grandmother was incredibly warm, and she had strong hands from years of working. She was almost a character out of a Hans Christian Andersen fable. And my grandfather was rough and mysterious in that typically Eastern European way.

Whenever we drove down to New Jersey to visit my Polish grandparents, we would get so excited. We used to count down the days. *Three more days! Two more days!* I remember every time we arrived at their house, my grandmother would be waiting for us outside on the porch. Every single time. This was before the era of cell phones and the drive was hours long, so she couldn't possibly have known at what exact time we would arrive. Whenever we pulled up, she would run down her landing, passing the Virgin Mary statue that had been painted and repainted a million times, speaking in Polish, and then she would hug us and cry because she had missed us so much. She spoke Polish to my father and soft broken English to us. Even if it wasn't perfect, I understood everything she was saying because it went beyond words. My grandmother spoke with her loving eyes, and she spoke through the food she made us, too. During our visits, she would feed us tremendous amounts of Polish food and special little candies with liquor inside.

Whereas my Italian grandparents were more Americanized, my Polish grandparents were not. My grandmother never learned to write in English. The last time I saw her she gave me a check and scribbled there was her name, Mary Cinkala. The signature is tenuous, as if she wasn't accustomed to writing. I look at that check and think about how hard it must have been for her to leave Poland as a young girl with little education and start over in America in the hopes of creating a better future.

For many years, my grandmother worked as a maid for wealthy people in New York City. She used to save the pantyhose her bosses threw away and fashion them into dolls and sell the dolls on the Brooklyn Bridge for extra cash. At the end of her life, when she was dying, she said, "Dorinda, you've become one of the women whose pantyhose I used to sell on the Brooklyn Bridge." She was very proud. My life, to her, represented an American dream.

When my siblings and I were growing up, my parents were determined to make us as American as possible. They didn't teach us

Italian or Polish. There was an American flag firmly planted in the front yard. But culturally, we were very much an immigrant family. We stuck together; we did whatever we could to make money; we didn't forget where we'd come from.

Food was love in our family, and I have endless memories of watching my mother standing at the counter baking or sautéing meat at the stove. She cooked dinner every single night at the same time—while teaching me lessons about life. If my mother was a teacher, then the kitchen was her classroom.

One day, pen and paper in hand, I said, "Mom, I want you to tell me your lasagna recipe."

"There's nothing to write down," my mother said. "It's not about what's on a piece of paper. It's about what you see while you're watching me."

This was how my mother had learned from her mother, and this was how I taught Hannah when she asked me about lasagna. I repeated to her what had been repeated to me. "It's more of a feeling than a recipe," I said. Because there had never been a written recipe for that lasagna. It was more like a short story passed down from generation to generation.

As my mother taught me how to cook, she was also teaching me about life. I remember her rolling out a pie dough and saying, "Everything you need to know about life happens in the kitchen. We solve problems when we're cooking. We communicate when we're cooking; we nurture and nourish ourselves with our food. We come to the table when we're happy. We come to the table when we're sad.

But we always come to the dinner table, no matter where we are in our lives."

After my grandmother died, my mother went home and cooked and welcomed people into the house. I'm sure what she really wanted to do was hide in her room and cry, but that wasn't an option. She just kept moving forward. Death, after all, was part of life. When I was a kid, when she used to say, "People are born and people die," I thought it was cold. But now I see how incredibly strong she was. In bad times and in good times, she did her tasks and kept a schedule, and it was the glue that held us together.

By watching my mother, I learned that if I just kept doing the next right thing, then life would keep unfolding. I still think this today. Having a routine is healthy. It creates stability. And it's very simple. Just do the next right thing. That's it. If you keep doing the next right thing, you'll eventually move forward in the right way.

Recently, Hannah said to me, "Mom, you cook all the time, but you don't like eating that much." And that's true. When no one is around, I eat a tuna fish sandwich or a can of soup. For me, making food is about togetherness and tradition. It's a way to show love. And it's correct what my mother said. No matter what is happening in our lives, we always come back to the dinner table.

When Richard died, I went home and my mother cooked, just as she's been doing all her life. She cooked with the same pans I'd been seeing since childhood. We ate with the same forks and sat at the same table, and the comfort of this routine gave me peace. I thought, *I can move forward because this is still here. I am going to be okay.*

The dinner table is like a situation room for our family. We laugh; we cry; we scream; we get into fights and make up. We eat and talk and eat and talk. I'll be honest: I never really detached from my parents. A lot of people leave home and move far away and barely talk to their parents. When I go home, I'm like a kid again, and I feel lucky to say that this is true.

When we were young, our parents were deeply committed to us having the brightest future possible and essential to that was Berkshire School, a boarding school just outside our town. There's a funny story about when my mom first went there to request a catalogue. When the admissions counselor asked if she had any children interested in applying, she responded, "Absolutely!" What she didn't mention was that the child in question was Johnny and he was two years old. You needed to be in the ninth grade to start at Berkshire School.

At fourteen, I was accepted to Berkshire School as a day student. On the first day, I remember looking at these private school kids and thinking they were just different. They dressed differently, spoke differently, and seemed to live in a different world. It was a world I knew nothing about. These people seemed refined, and I decided that I wanted to be like them. But I soon realized that I didn't understand their lives at all.

When a new friend asked me what I was doing for spring break, I said, "I don't know." I thought, *What does that even mean? What else would I be doing during spring break other than staying home and picking up a few shifts at Friendly's?*

Up until that point, I didn't even realize that going on vacation for spring break was an option. The friend sort of chuckled at me, and I thought to myself, *I am never going to say, "I don't know," to that question again.* I decided I would rather pretend I had somewhere fabulous to go than get laughed at. I wanted to belong. I wanted to be refined. And since I didn't feel very refined, I would fake it. I would create a character for myself, and eventually, I would become that character. When in doubt, fake it till you make it!

My mother used to say, "Have you ever noticed that people marry who they hang around with? It's like schools of fish. They stay together. So if you want to get out of your school of fish, you need to make changes. If you're swimming with the minnows, but you really want to be a shark, then you better figure out how to join the sharks." The other thing she used to say all the time was, "If you want to catch an elephant, then don't go to the ocean. Go to the jungle."

Berkshire School was the first time I went to the jungle. I was exposed to a world of privilege and ease, and I found it baffling in the beginning. I remember one day I went to a friend's house and she said, "It's time to do the *New York Times* crossword puzzle."

What? A crossword puzzle? Weren't we supposed to be cooking or cleaning or doing something tangibly productive? The first time I heard the word "brunch," I was confused. What the hell was brunch?

The deeper I got into the jungle, the more I wanted to live there forever. I was in awe of how many Ralph Lauren sweaters these kids had and grateful we wore a uniform to school so I could pretend that maybe, at home, I had those sweaters, too. I got a boyfriend from a nearby private school and new friends. One of them lived in Italy during the summers. Another friend had Chanel lipstick. Chanel! Can you imagine? Until then, I'd only ever seen my mother's Revlon tubes up close. A Chanel lipstick at the time, just so you know, cost about $25! And a Revlon cost $4.99. I remember this because I used to save my waitressing tips to buy them for myself.

I want to talk a little more about friendships because over the course of my life they've played a very important role. When I was very young, my brothers and sister were my main playmates, but I was also very social with the kids at school. I was always rounding up friends to play games and chitter-chatter. I liked having people around and I liked interacting. My childhood friendships were a lot like my adult friendships. I had a lot of acquaintances, but I wasn't very popular. I had a few main friends and a bunch of other people I knew loosely.

It wasn't until I went to Berkshire School that I started to develop deep friendships. My best friend there was Livia, and like me, Livia was a high achiever. We were more focused on exploring what lay ahead of us in life than we were in boys. We had goals.

Livia's parents were Italian, but unlike my ethnic family, hers was wealthy. Livia was the coolest friend I'd ever had until that point. In more ways than one, we were total opposites. I was blond with blue eyes. Livia had dark features and was incredibly elegant. My parents were middle class. Livia's parents had an apartment in New York, and during the summers they traveled to Italy. I thought that was exotic and adventurous. It was so far beyond the bubble I knew.

The first time I went to New York City was not with Livia. It was on a church bus trip with my parents. I'll tell you about my first impressions of that in a second. What I want to tell you about now is how, near the end of high school, I started going on weekend trips to New York with Livia and her parents, to stay in their apartment in the city. It amazed me. We went to restaurants and shopping and on walks in Central Park. Livia wasn't a visitor in the city. She treated it like home. Livia was the first person who showed me that New York wasn't an unreachable place. It could be the place you actually lived.

Livia was fearless and intensely academic, as was I, and as time went on, our friendship became a little competitive. At the end of high school, we lost touch, not because we didn't like each other anymore, but because when I left home I needed to redefine myself and this meant letting go of my old environment and a lot of the people who were in it.

Livia and my other new friends at Berkshire School really opened my eyes to a new way of living. They had what seemed like endless amounts of free time. Their lives seemed so effortless and beautiful and abundant, and I was just in awe. To be like them became a goal that I was constantly striving for. Doing well in French wasn't about doing well in French; it was about the possibility of traveling to Europe after I graduated. I involved myself in as many activities as possible. I joined the student council. I became an athlete. I got perfect grades. It became all about being the *best*.

My mom was incredibly supportive. This dream of achieving something more was one that we both shared. But when I chose lacrosse instead of tennis, I could tell she was disappointed. "Tennis is a sport you can play for the rest of your life," she said. "And it's what established people play."

Along with the certainty that I was going to leave Great Barrington and become successful, there was a lot of doubt. I always feared that I wouldn't make it. I always feared that people would figure out I didn't belong. I was fearful all the time. At some point, my goals switched the cart with the horse and the cart got ahead of me. I was no longer the driving force that was pulling my life forward; I was being dragged backwards by my unrealistic expectations of myself. "I need to do my best" became "I am not enough and never will be enough." There will always be someone prettier, or smarter, or skinnier, so the dream of being the best went from a dream to a nightmare, a journey to nowhere that was exhausting and unhealthy.

As a consequence of all the pressure I put on myself, I developed an eating disorder. I exercised excessively and counted every calorie. The weight loss made me feel like I was in control. It gave me a sense of certainty. If I didn't eat, then I lost weight. If I kept pushing myself, then I would get to where I wanted to be.

It got pretty bad. All I would eat were watery vegetables and I would go on five-mile runs every day. I developed a layer of fur all over my body—a common side effect of anorexia. My mother was frantic and felt totally powerless. It was the first time she couldn't fix my problem. Being thin wasn't just about looking like a model in a magazine. On some level, it made me feel *special*. I enjoyed my mother obsessing about my weight because it meant that all of her attention and concern was on me. For better or for worse, there was a part of me that wanted to be taken care of by my mother in the doting way I had been when I was little. When you're about to be swallowed up by a vast sea, you're not afraid to swim farther away from the shore if it means you can grab hold of a buoy.

One night during dinner when I was doing everything but eating my food—cutting it up, moving it around my plate, pulling the bread off my burger, trying to imperceptibly tuck the meat into my napkin when no one was looking so I could throw it out later—my mother lost it. She stood up, and with a force that was more urgent than it was angry she shouted, "You better snap out of it, Dorinda, or you're gonna squander everything you've worked for! You'll either end up in the hospital or I will put you there if I have to."

My mom had reached the end of her rope. The reality of how my eating disorder could hurt my future and separate me from my family was worse than the twenty pounds that separated my old body from my new one. I slowly got myself healthy again, but the longing for that feeling of control that I had when I was anorexic lingered beyond the weight gain. Eating disorders are demons that are attracted to a specific flavor of vulnerability and insecurity—and those insecurities never *really* go away.

After letting go of my eating disorder, I put my energy into my future. I kept moving forward, and I kept my big dreams. It would take me a long time to realize that this—the determination to constantly move forward—was something I could use to my benefit. Hard work and determination in the pursuit of my goals became a huge part of my value system as I got older.

When you're operating from a mentality of scarcity, it's tough to see the bigger picture, particularly when you lack a sense of what the world looks like outside your neighborhood. For many, many years, I couldn't see the bigger picture at all. I could only see the next step in front of me. At seventeen years old, though, I came face-to-face with the big picture I was meant to see: New York.

The first time I went to the Big Apple was with my parents, as I mentioned. It was on a church trip to see the Rockettes at Christmas. It was a very big deal. We booked the trip in June, and I spent the next six months looking forward to going to this mystical place I'd only ever seen on television.

In December, I boarded the Peter Pan Bus with my parents, and when we drove over the bridge I was just dazzled. Sometimes you have high expectations of a place and then the reality of it is a letdown. Well, New York wasn't that at all. If anything, it was better than I'd imagined. The minute I saw all those bustling people and felt all that energy, I knew that this was where I belonged.

Technically, I barely stepped foot in Manhattan that day. The bus drove us straight to the Rockettes performance and straight back to Massachusetts afterwards. And my mother insisted on holding my hand for the short time we were out on the sidewalk, because she was convinced that I would be kidnapped. To her, the city was like Alcatraz, full of thieves and rapists. "This is where the alligators live," she said.

"Mom, I'm going to live here one day," I told her.

"No, you're not, Dorinda. You can move to Boston, but not here."

My mother was right about almost everything, but I knew that when it came to me and my destiny in New York she was wrong.

Madonna once did an appearance on *American Bandstand*, which was a show I watched religiously. When Dick Clark asked her what she planned to do next, she said, "Rule the world."

I didn't know how I was going to get back to New York City or what I was going to do when I arrived, but I knew that one day it would happen and that when it did it would feel like I had conquered the world.

Fool me once, shame on me.
Fool me twice . . . don't fool me twice.

Chapter Three

THE BIGGER PICTURE

As we all know, life doesn't always give us what we want, but we have to take what we're given and make it work to our advantage.

At the end of high school, I applied to college. I'd excelled at Berkshire School. I'd joined all the groups and gotten good grades. I'd done my very best. For my classmates, money wasn't a factor in choosing a college, but for me, it was. It was understood that I would attend the college that awarded me the most scholarship money.

I applied to Franklin & Marshall because my brother Johnny had gone there on scholarship, and I applied to Boston College, which was where I really wanted to go. Everyone at Berkshire School wanted to go to Boston College in those days. It was prestigious and it was especially appealing to me because it was only two hours away from home, whereas Franklin & Marshall was a whopping five hours away in Pennsylvania.

Boston College rejected me. I was so discouraged. But did I choose to sit back and quietly accept this rejection? No, I did not. I made an enormous fortune cookie with a fortune inside that said: "DC belongs at BC." My mother drove me down to Boston College and I left this fortune cookie with the president. Shortly after that, I was put on a wait list. I thought I had a good chance.

Maybe I would have eventually made it in as a student at Boston College, but I would never find out, because while I was waiting, Franklin & Marshall accepted me and offered me a scholarship. My father had a stern conversation with me. "You're going to Franklin and Marshall and that's it."

I was incredibly upset. I'd tried so hard. I'd overachieved. And meanwhile, classmates of mine who'd achieved far less slipped into Boston College and other schools because their wealthy parents had contacts there or had gone to those schools themselves. For the first time, I truly felt like life wasn't fair. I'd been raised to believe that if you did all the right things you were going to be okay, but at this moment I realized that wasn't always true. The world did not always reward your good efforts. But it did always reward wealth and connections.

I was sullen as my parents drove me to Pennsylvania, and I was heartbroken when my mother said, "See you at Thanksgiving." Thanksgiving was months away! How was I not going to see my parents until Thanksgiving? As I watched my parents drive away, I was completely overwhelmed, thinking, *What have I done?*

For the first semester, I was depressed. I missed home all the time. I'd never spent the night anywhere other than my parents' house and my grandparents' house, and now I had to share a dorm room with a nutty girl I didn't know. From the very first night, she was bringing guys back to our room. It was just foreign to me. I was still a virgin then and used to the cozy, safe environment of my childhood home. Once a week, I would call my parents from the dorm pay phone, but we couldn't talk for long because it was expensive. On every call, I cried and told them about how much I hated college.

Although I was terribly homesick at first, I slowly came to understand that I had to engage. Other than Christmas break, spring break, and summer, I couldn't afford to go back and forth from Lancaster to Great Barrington, so I had to find a new support system at school. I made friends with many new interesting people, a lot of whom were different from me. Some of them were in sororities. Others were more artsy. At college, I learned to be open to new people and situations, and I really blossomed.

I was always on the go, and even though I had to work while I was in college and keep up my grades because I had a scholarship, I always found time to socialize. Franklin & Marshall is a smaller school. It had about twelve hundred students when I was there. Fraternities and sororities were big and each house attracted a unique group. I was good at going between groups, although I was probably most drawn to Chi Phi because its members were preppy, a lot like the kids at Berkshire School. They had formals and cocktail parties they liked to call smokers. And they played preppy sports like lacrosse, tennis, and squash.

I arrived at Franklin & Marshall with a lot of the preppiness I'd picked up from Livia and Berkshire School, but at heart, I was kind of a hippie. I loved Crosby, Stills & Nash. I had hair down to my belly button. I wore wild outfits, like an IZOD shirt with a denim skirt and a bunch of multicolored scarves.

One day in the quad, a fellow student came up to me with a huge smile on her face and said, "Hi, my name is June. I like your skirt." June became my first deep and long-lasting friend. I was drawn to her because she had the same childlike sense of wonder and silliness that I had. We were both sort of immature, and when I was with her I felt like I was home. June had attended a prep school like I had and she was a hippie, but an elegant one. She resembled a young Candice Bergen. Smart and kind, June was a mix of a fairy princess and flower child. She was ethereal and wacky, but in a grounded, relatable way.

June and I loved to sit in the quad and talk for hours. One of our favorite things to do was exercise—and boy, did we exercise. We walked excessively; we worked out to Jane Fonda tapes; we swam endless laps (while pausing to chat) in the Olympic-sized pool at the school gym. After, we'd go to the salad bar at Wendy's, where we'd raid the carrots section. The more I got to know her, the more I realized how much we had in common. Neither of us had ever had a serious boyfriend, we liked the same music, we had eclectic tastes that set us apart from the norm, and we were both artsy. We loved painting, knitting, beading, and art.

June is still a big presence in my life. Together, we've lived through many jobs and boyfriends and adventures. We were at each other's weddings; we welcomed each other's babies. After my divorce and Richard's death, June was there to comfort me.

Looking back, it was a blessing I didn't go to Boston College, because if I had, I never would have met June. I would have gone home every weekend. So, this is a good example of how what I thought was initially a failure turned out to be the best thing that could have happened.

My friends, and especially June, started to feel like my family, and I began to really enjoy the communal aspect of college. Back then, nobody was hiding in their dorm room scrolling through Instagram. We were in the quad or the student center hanging out or in class or at the library studying.

The work-hard-play-hard mentality at Franklin & Marshall was right up my alley—and it was kind of an epiphany. I had always worked hard, but now I could have fun, too. I got good grades and took my classes very seriously, because, as I was the first girl in our family to go to college, there was no way I was going to let myself or my parents down. And in addition to all that hard work, I also learned to have some fun.

One night at the dorms, I met a member of the Chi Phi fraternity named Billy. Billy was preppy and cool and he played the saxophone, and I quickly fell madly in love with him. I was so innocent back then that I thought when you fell in love you would get married and have children and build a life together. That's what my parents had done, so those were my plans for myself, too.

I've heard a lot of people talk about their first love, the one they never got over. Well, that love for me is Billy. I think I still love him, even today, maybe because he was the first. From the moment I saw Billy, I loved him.

Before Billy, I'd never been boy crazy. And I didn't consider my sexuality much at all because it just didn't exist in my house growing up. The idea of losing my virginity was a big deal. For the rest of freshman year, Billy and I dated, but I refused to sleep with him. He made fun of me for that, but I also think it made him want me more.

By the time I went home after freshman year, I loved college so much that I couldn't wait to go back and see Billy and my friends. That summer and every other summer during college, I focused all my energy on working and making money. I waitressed at the Red Lion Inn, and let me tell you, I was not a passive waitress. I would take every single shift that opened up. I'd offer a deal to the waitresses who I knew were single mothers: "You can go home to your babysitter. I'll pick up your table. And we can split the tip. What do you think?"

When that first summer was over, I went back to Franklin & Marshall with all the money I'd saved and reunited with Billy, who was not only the sexiest man I'd ever seen but also my best friend. I was just crazy for him, but sadly, so were all the other women at college.

During my sophomore year, I finally slept with Billy. It was the beginning of the end. After that, things changed. We didn't break up, but we never became an item either. No one could figure out if we were together or not, including us. It was tumultuous and passionate and ultimately not very healthy. We'd break up and then we would get back together. It would go astoundingly well for a while, and then he'd disappear from my life.

What Billy did give me was an appreciation for sex and love. Sex was fun. And love, when it was complicated, was a gamble. On the one hand, the pull I felt toward Billy was intoxicating. On the other hand, him not wanting to commit to me was painful!

Billy was a year older, so he left school before I did. I was crushed and angry that he didn't love me enough, and so without good judgment I started dating one of his fraternity brothers. Oops! This wasn't the end of me and Billy, though. For the next many years, all the way up until I met my first husband, Ralph, Billy and I would continue to see each other on and off. The nature of our relationship never changed. It was always passionate. And it was always an absolute disaster.

When I arrived at college, I was sporting a bohemian, hippieish look. Over the years, I added a preppy spice to it. By the end of college, there was lots of Laura Ashley in my wardrobe and, of course, Ralph Lauren. I saved up for an entire summer to buy two cable-knit Ralph Lauren sweaters. One was gray and one was hot pink and they were the chicest thing ever. Other favorite staples of that time were my Gloria Vanderbilt denim skirt and my Calvin Klein jeans.

On top of these classic basics, I layered on statement necklaces and headbands. I'd been making headbands since I was a kid. I would take all my mother's hangers and break them up and bend them into headbands and sell them. I also sewed my own clothes. And I used to save up for *Vogue* subscriptions and then tear the pages out and make these enormous idea books, which were basically like vision boards.

Vision boards illustrate what you want in the future, but somehow, despite the fact that I had the answer right in front of me, I still couldn't see it. I spent all four years at college thinking I would be a lawyer. Even as I sat there sewing bandanas together in my dorm room to make a skirt, I was still planning to go to law school. I thought it was a logical choice. The law interested me, and I was also interested in financial security. I also thought that becoming a lawyer would mean I had one of the most powerful jobs a woman could have, and that's what I wanted: to become a powerful woman who'd achieved her own success and who answered to no one.

But right after I graduated, I realized that my plans were wrong. I had no interest in studying law. Obviously, my future was in fashion. I applied and got into the Macy's buyers program, hoping it would take me to New York. Unfortunately, I got stationed in New Jersey instead, but that was okay. At least I was getting closer. My father bought me a Subaru and off I went to Far Hills, New Jersey, to live with my Polish aunt and uncle and their young daughter. I was happy to have this comfortable home base, but it was also such a stark contrast to my communal college life. I remember one night in Far Hills I was invited to go bowling. *Bowling? Where was the cocktail party?*

Along with the goal of starting a career in fashion, I also wanted to meet a respectable man. And I definitely didn't think that man was at a bowling alley. He was in New York. Whenever I had free time, I would ride the train into the city to see friends. Slowly, I was building a foundation in my city, even though I didn't live there yet.

The Macy's program was intense. In twelve weeks, we were going to learn everything there was to know about retail so that afterwards we'd get hired as buyers. For the first half of the day, we'd be in class in Morristown, and for the second half, we'd go to different Macy's locations to get hands-on experience. I learned how to manage a floor, how to keep track of an inventory, and how to merchandise. I also learned about how to deal with customers. If somebody came in to return a shirt with spaghetti sauce on it that they'd clearly been wearing for five years, I'd ask, "Did you wear this?" If the customer said no, then I processed the return, because the customer is always right.

After finishing the Macy's program, I decided to move to New York. First, though, I needed a job. I went to a temp agency, as one did in those days, and was placed at Grey Advertising as a reception-ist. Advertising was huge back then, and Grey managed some of the biggest campaigns. The offices were full of slick, creative men and women who came up with breathtaking ideas while chain-smoking cigarettes. I'd never been around women like that before. They were tough, and I was in awe of them.

I was a fantastic receptionist. I got to meet and greet people, my favorite thing, and man (or woman) the switchboard. Eventually, I became a runner, which meant that I would run material from office to office. They paid me almost nothing, but I didn't care. I loved the atmosphere, and I loved working inside the Lipstick Building, which is an iconic building on the East Side of Manhattan. It just seemed so glamorous.

Through a friend at Grey, I got a cheap room on the Upper East Side. It was a fourth-floor walk-up on 78th and First and my roommate was an opera singer. In some ways, she was like my first roommate at college. She'd bring random men home to sleep at the apartment. Now that I had my own room, I'd barricade the door with my dresser just in case. One morning, there was a naked man standing in my kitchen and he was just talking to me like everything was fine and normal. I thought, *This is not normal!* It was bizarre and a little bit scary.

In that apartment building, there was a very old woman who lived across the hall. She was so old that she couldn't get up and down the stairs, so she used to ask me to bring her food. I didn't have the extra cash to be buying her food, but I did it anyway because I felt so sorry for her. When she opened the door, I could see that her apartment was filthy inside. It was not the kind of New York future that I wanted for myself.

Even though my first apartment wasn't the best, I was just so happy to finally be in the city. Plus, I had no expectations of living well back then. I just needed a place to lay my head. As you can probably imagine, my parents were less than thrilled at the prospect of me living in New York (they thought it was scary, dirty, and awful), so I told them less about the negative aspects and focused more on the positives. I said, "It's amazing. I love it. My apartment's in a great area. Everyone is so nice. I never go out at night." Of course, a lot of this was completely fabricated. The reality of New York was harsh and daunting. But it was full of enough opportunity and excitement to keep me there.

All the kids I knew who'd moved to New York after college were scraping by, like me, and it was possible to live inexpensively. The Upper East Side was teeming with cheap restaurants and bars and kids who'd just graduated. We were out all the time, bustling with the city, and going home to sleep on our Jennifer convertible beds, and we thought it was fabulous. New York was gritty back then, and if you were a respectable woman you didn't take the subway to work. You took a cab. But we couldn't afford cabs. I solved this riddle by collecting a bunch of people and then piling us into the same cab to go to work. Since we all worked in midtown, it was easy. We'd meet in the morning around 79th Street and be driven down to the 50s like little sardines.

We did everything together in those days. Living on the Upper East Side was, in many ways, an extension of college. We lived and worked in the same neighborhoods. We had a weekly list of all the happy hours to hit. We were always running into one another on the street. Back then, the only way to communicate was on a landline. The first thing we did when we got home was run to the Memorex answering machine to see if we had any messages. Can you imagine how exciting it was to get a message? When I would press the button and hear "You have three new messages," it was like the voice of God was talking to me. *Three* new messages?

After about four months at Grey, I saw an ad in *Women's Wear Daily*. Liz Claiborne was hiring. Liz Claiborne was everything back then, a real industry leader, and I decided that I absolutely had to get the job.

I prepared carefully, as I always do. Preparation is key. How are you going to get what you want if you roll in late with no plan? Pure luck? Luck is nice, but it's not a very strong plan. A huge part of preparation, especially when you're hoping to get a job in the fashion industry, is presentation. People make snap judgments based on what they see, so you have to make your first impression stellar.

Before the Liz Claiborne interview, I went to TJ Maxx and bought a cool Perry Ellis suit I couldn't really afford, but I knew this was a place to throw down some money. You have to invest in your look, right? You have to spend money to make money sometimes. I paired the suit with a white Oxford shirt and fake pearl earrings from Ann Taylor. I thought I looked very chic.

On the day of the interview, the Liz Claiborne office was full of other women like me. The receptionist called name after name after name and I watched these other women enter the doors to be interviewed by the boss, whom I'll call X here.

I waited.

And I waited.

And then the receptionist came out and said, "Interviews are over."

"What? But I want to interview!"

"Sorry," the receptionist said.

I went home discouraged. Then, in the morning, I got dressed in my outfit again and went right back to the Liz Claiborne office and said, "I have an interview with X."

"I don't see you on the list," the receptionist said.

I pretended to be confused. The receptionist sent me to HR, where I pretended to be confused again, and I ended up back in the Liz Claiborne waiting room, just waiting.

The following day, I did the same thing.

Finally, one day after that, X walked out and said, "Who are you?"

"I'm Dorinda Cinkala and I'm here to interview for the job," I said.

She looked me up and down.

"I'll give you ten minutes."

I told her that I was a hard worker, that I would take any job, and that I was open to learning new skills. I talked about how being a former waitress had taught me about sales. I was charming, witty, I could multitask, and I was always on time. Also, I knew how to make myself look attractive, which in the eighties was very important.

Well, I must have made a good first impression on X, because at the end of those ten minutes I was hired.

Like New York City itself, the Liz Claiborne job was fantastically glamorous—with a less fabulous underbelly. The best part of working at Liz Claiborne was seeing Liz Claiborne herself. She'd come in, in her crisp shirts and her slacks and her big glasses, and say, "Hello, girls." It was amazing to me, as was the clothing allowance I got. Can you imagine getting an allowance to buy Liz Claiborne clothes? I couldn't have been happier. My wardrobe upgrade was great for work and it meant that I looked snazzier in my personal life, too.

I was hired as a wholesaler in the women's wear department, so my job consisted of booking appointments with department stores and small clothing shops and selling to them. Back then, you formed personal relationships with your buyers and if they liked you then it was pretty much guaranteed that they'd buy from you if it was within their budget. I was a great salesperson. I love people and I can get interested in anything. If you told me about your dog, I could ask you questions about your dog for hours. Really, I learned everything I needed to know about sales from my years as a waitress. I could sell hamburgers just like I could sell raincoats. It's all about being a good talker and coming across as confident. At the Red Lion Inn, I used to take orders without writing them down. Once in a while, a customer would say to me, "Shouldn't you write that down?"

"Absolutely not," I'd say. "Do you think I'd forget an order like yours? Come on."

I'd offer that same type of assurance to the buyers I worked with in retail. People trusted me, because I didn't lie to them. I would say, "This raincoat is not worth your time, but that one is." If you want to be a credible source, then you can't lie. You have to speak the truth.

Along with the sales part of the sales job I'd been hired for, I had other duties, like brushing and braiding a manager's hair. Yes, in the mornings, while she did her makeup, I would brush her hair and braid it. Back then, this was a totally acceptable thing to ask an underling to do. I also somehow had to walk her dog before work, and sometimes on Saturday mornings she'd call and ask me to do her grocery shopping. And I used to babysit her kids for free. I never said no. I accepted the terms of the job because I wanted to work at Liz Claiborne more than I wanted to risk the possibility of getting fired for complaining.

I eventually left the opera singer and moved in with some friends from college. One of them was very socially connected, so she started getting us invited to all these great parties. We worked like animals during the day, and then at night we'd go to our favorite places. The Racquet and Tennis Club was a members-only men's club that hosted cocktail parties and fabulous events. The Pen & Pencil was once referred to as the "ultimate Mad Men bar." And then there was the Carlyle Hotel, home of famous Bemelmans Bar, which was filled by Upper East Siders like me. Even though working and making money were my priorities, I was definitely on the prowl. And I didn't want some fling with a guy from a dive bar. I wanted a serious relationship.

In many ways, I had grown up a lot by this point, but sometimes I still made mistakes. After working at Liz Claiborne for about two years, I got a huge bonus. Did I put it in my savings account for later? No. I went to the Surf Club, where my friend Tiger, who ran the VIP room, let me slip in. And then I decided to buy drinks for everyone at the bar.

"Drinks for everyone! I got a bonus!"

Right after I made this announcement, I felt sick to my stomach. And then on Monday, I called the bank and basically found out I had no money left in my account. I called my parents and said, "I messed up."

"Come home for a while," they said. "We'll send a bus ticket."

So that's what I did. I went home to Great Barrington. It was important to go back home, lick my wounds, regroup, and make some money waitressing before venturing back to the city again. I always wanted to support myself and be independent. The great thing about my parents is that they've always kept the door open for me. When I went back, they didn't judge me. To them, I hadn't failed. It was just part of the process. I'd fallen off the horse and now I was going to figure out how to get on the horse again.

I immediately got my old waitressing job back at the Red Lion Inn and started saving money so I could get back to New York as soon as possible. I also decided to get braces. My teeth were not very straight and I thought, *What better time to get braces than while I'm hiding out in Massachusetts? Also, what better time to become an aerobics instructor?*

One day, I saw an ad for a training certification at the YMCA and signed up. I'd been aerobicizing with Jane Fonda's VHS tapes for years and I'd always loved fitness, so it made sense. After the certification program, I started teaching in Great Barrington at a hair salon with a friend. It was the best side hustle ever. I could stay fit, wear fun spandex, and make a nice supplementary income.

After a year in Great Barrington, I had enough money saved to return to New York. I got a new apartment on the Upper East Side and a new job at a clothing company called British Khaki. Just as I'd done at Liz Claiborne, I worked as a wholesaler, and I loved it. On the weekends, I taught aerobics at the Vertical Club. As a side hustle to my side hustle, I started selling the mix tapes I used in class. As usual, if there was a way to make money, then I was going to make it.

After getting kicked back home because I'd been financially careless, I made the decision that that was never going to happen again. It was a painful lesson, but it was necessary. When I moved to New York the second time, I took a percentage of every paycheck I got and put it in a savings account. I still do this today. Having a cushion not only keeps you sane—it also builds wealth.

I have always been a woman who loves to work. I knew that being a good worker was the way to move forward. Sure, I wanted to find a successful husband, but the number one goal was making myself successful. In the meantime, I would make myself *appear* successful. Just as I would curate a list of clothes to sell to buyers, I curated my personal look. Liz Claiborne. British Khaki. Ralph Lauren. Ann Taylor. If you'd seen me from across the room at the Racquet Club, you probably would have thought I was a successful person, and that was the whole point.

At twenty-five, I knew that if I kept working and kept putting myself in the right environments while wearing the right clothes, then I would eventually become the successful woman I looked like on the outside. All I had to do was stay the course and keep going and one day it was going to work out.

In the meantime, I was determined not to waste time dating people who were wrong for me. I knew what kind of man I wanted, and I wasn't going to settle for anything less. Specifically, what I wanted was a responsible, loving partner who valued family, religion, and finances like I did. I was done dating for the sake of dating. I wanted to find a husband. I hear so many women complaining about their partners—but they have *chosen* those partners! If you know you want a steak, you have to order a steak. You cannot order a hamburger and then be upset when it turns out not to be a steak.

The other important thing to remember is that you cannot turn a hamburger into a steak. It's never going to happen. You have to accept people as they are. Trying to change them is a horrible way to spend your time. So, if you're single and still waiting for your ideal partner to enter your life, that's good. Keep waiting. Don't settle for less. I waited for a long time, and then I finally met Ralph Lynch. He was exactly the type of man I'd always dreamed of—but better.

We met at a wedding. I knew the bride; he knew the groom. After Ralph spoke to me for the first time, I said, "Oh my God, you have a real British accent."

"No," he said, "it's a Scottish accent."

I was mesmerized and impressed by Ralph's accent. More, I was amazed that he not only had a Scottish accent, he'd also literally grown up in Scotland. He also worked at Prudential Bank as an investment banker. *And* he had gone to Columbia. *And* he'd been a rugby player!

Ralph wasn't slick like a lot of the investment bankers I'd met around town. There was nothing slippery about him. He was mellow and grounded and handsome and so polite. Next to Ralph, I felt like a lady. I remember standing there under this very tall man thinking, *This is someone I can really sink my teeth into.* By the way, I was still wearing my braces when we met.

I knew from the very beginning that Ralph would make a good father, but I wouldn't tell him that for a while. That night, we talked and danced and had a fantastic time and at the end he asked me out on a date.

Life isn't about finding yourself.
It's about creating yourself.

Chapter Four

DORINDA LYNCH

On our first date, Ralph picked me up in a town car. Can you imagine? For a woman who couldn't afford cab fare, this was miraculous. Then it got even crazier. Between us in the backseat was a box. Well, Ralph opened this box and inside the box was a phone. A *car* phone! Ralph made a call and then he was casually talking into the receiver as we drove through Manhattan. I just could not believe that it was a real phone. In a *car*.

Ralph took me to a beautiful dinner that night, and afterwards I took him to an Irish bar that I liked. The band started playing "The Unicorn" by the Irish Rovers, which goes: "Green alligators and long necked geese / Some humpty-back camels and some chimpanzees . . ." If you don't know this song, there's a famous dance that goes along with it. Well, I got up on the bar and started dancing and he thought, *This is the type of person I need in my life.*

The more I got to know Ralph, the more I liked him. He was a solid human being with a dry sense of humor that I found hilarious.

Ralph was clever, and he spoke in a deadpan monotone that just cracked me up. Ralph wasn't fast and loose like a lot of the guys I knew. He wasn't the type to sleep around. He didn't have an agenda. He was a loyal, hardworking man who always tried to do the right thing when it came to the people he loved. And, on top of being a great human, he happened to have all the outside things that made me swoon, like a big job at a bank and a car phone.

In the late eighties, investment bankers had the world at their feet. They had drivers. They had beautiful apartments. They had expense accounts. They were making tremendous amounts of money. Dating Ralph opened up a new world to me, and it was a world of elegance and opulence. Gone were the happy hours and Chinese restaurants that served free wine with their meals. We now went to grown-up restaurants. I got used to driving around in the town car. I no longer wanted to get my toenails done on Second Avenue and walk around in disposable flip-flops. I wanted to dress more nicely and be more refined.

Hanging around with his friends was a revelation to me in so many ways. It was kind of the same revelation I'd had at Berkshire School, but bigger. The host of a Christmas party we went to had a tree ferried up to his rooftop apartment with a crane! It was just decadent beyond belief. I was struck by how at ease Ralph's friends seemed and how nobody looked tired. When you had money, you weren't anxious all the time. You weren't scared. You slept more soundly and had fewer wrinkles.

Unlike Richard, whom I'd meet many years later, Ralph wasn't showy. He was quiet, conservative, and responsible. He was the guy you wanted to be with if something went wrong. If Ralph Lynch had been on the *Titanic*, he'd be the person who'd get you to safety, and he wouldn't make a big deal about it either.

On the outside, we were very different. I was silly and loud and Ralph was reserved. But ultimately, we were two people from a similar background who wanted the same things out of life. His mother had opened a hair salon and worked hard to raise and support three boys. Ralph and I were both quite traditional in certain ways. We were committed to each other. With Ralph, it wasn't a passionate love affair; it was a true partnership.

After we'd been dating for about a year, Ralph got a job offer at Lehman Brothers. Back then, it was all about merging domestic companies with overseas ones, and they would often send investment bankers abroad to make deals. Well, Ralph was thinking about transferring to the Hong Kong office, and he asked me to come with him.

"Yes!"

I didn't think twice. I had moved to New York City, I had a wonderful and successful boyfriend, and now we were going to live *abroad*. I'd only left the United States once, to backpack through Europe, and now I was going to *live* abroad? I thought it was the best thing that had ever happened to me. This was exactly what I had wanted. No, it was more than I had wanted; it was more than I had even thought to dream of. "Abroad," to me, was just so decadent and, quite frankly, still is. But I was naïve about it, too. It's not like I was a worldly woman. Consciously or subconsciously, I thought

"abroad" meant diving into a cartoon poster of the Eiffel Tower—
even though we were going to Asia. And I felt special—maybe too
special. During that time, if a friend said to me, "I'm moving to
Chicago," I would say, "That's nice. I am moving *abroad*."

My mother bawled her eyes out when I told her. In her mind,
it was like I had died. Remember, back then there were no cell
phones and no FaceTime. And you couldn't just pick up the phone
in China, punch in your phone number, and talk to someone in the
United States. Operators were involved. It was complicated. After
my mother finally stopped crying, she had questions. "You're moving to Hong Kong with a man who hasn't proposed to you?"

I'd prepared for this, because I knew my mother. Before calling
her with the news, I'd told Ralph that my parents were going to
freak out if we weren't engaged. Ralph and I knew we were in it for
the long haul anyway, so him getting me a placeholder ring (which
I still have and love) a bit earlier than expected wasn't that crazy. He
bought me a band so I would have something to show my parents,
and for the next few months we pretended to be engaged, with the
understanding that one day there would be a real proposal. It was
unconventional but in its own way incredibly romantic.

With a placeholder ring on my finger and Ralph by my side, I
quit my job, packed up my life, and hopped on a plane to China. I
just knew that this was it. This was the next big jump. This was going
to be so exciting.

Well, it turned out that my dreams of living abroad and the
reality of it were not aligned at all. I am not saying that Hong Kong

is a bad city, but it wasn't a place where I felt at home. First of all, it was like Mars. I couldn't speak the language, I didn't understand the customs, I was unfamiliar with the culture, and the city was enormous. You have to understand that I was still in my twenties and was totally naïve. To me, when I first moved to New York, it felt like I had moved to a different country. So you can imagine how Hong Kong felt: beyond foreign.

Ralph's brother had moved to Hong Kong first, so we stayed with him. Then we started the process of looking at beautiful apartments to rent. They were apartments with sweeping views of the Hong Kong harbor—the kinds of apartments that had a magical view of Hong Kong, a place I had only seen in films and pictures. *I am like a real-life princess*, I thought to myself. After brushing a manager's hair at Liz Claiborne, I now had a housekeeper who wanted to brush *my* hair. I didn't want her to, but I thought the offer was both bizarre and exciting.

Ralph worked for fifteen hours a day, so I soon found myself alone all the time, and with no friends. Exxon had a big presence in Hong Kong at that time, so there were a lot of Exxon wives, but they were older than me and had set lives with their husbands. I considered them to be Junior League–y country club women and I couldn't really relate to them. I missed home. I became terribly depressed. I was learning that living in the lap of luxury was nice, but it didn't necessarily solve all your problems.

One day, I got myself together and decided to take a fun day trip to Kowloon, a historical city that's a few miles away from Hong

Kong Island by boat. Sightseeing! Somebody had told me that it was a fabulous place to go. I got on the boat, I wandered around Kowloon for a little while, and then I decided it was time to go back to Hong Kong, but there was one big problem. Nobody spoke English in Kowloon. Unlike in Hong Kong, people in Kowloon were only speaking Mandarin. The harbor was full of what seemed like hundreds of boats. Which was the right one? I tried to ask people where to go, but nobody understood what I was saying. I wanted to cry. Intellectually I knew I would get home, but in the moment it was as though I were stranded on a desert island. Then, just as I was about to lose my mind, I was saved by a local woman who pointed at one of the boats and said, "Hong Kong."

After that trip to Kowloon, I mostly stayed in the apartment and I felt even more trapped and lonely than I had before. I lived in beautiful surroundings, but I found it very isolating. When Ralph would come home, I would just cry and cry. I felt so detached. I was lucky to have a partner like Ralph. Knowing how unhappy I was, Ralph asked to be transferred to London.

We did short stints in Australia, Paris, and Munich first, staying in each city for about a month while Ralph closed deals. Life in those cities felt like a vacation for me. When Ralph left for the office, I would set out as a tourist, swimming around the Great Barrier Reef at Hayman Island in Australia. I would watch old men play boules on the Place Dauphine. I had been to many of the European cities before, when I went backpacking in the summer before college, and yet I couldn't help but feel like I had never really *seen* them. Now

I was behind the curtain and living in a dazzling universe of five-star hotels. What I found, however, was that while these experiences were exciting and uplifting, they also came with a hint of melancholy. It was like a nostalgic sense of regret that drew me to the past and isolated me in the present at the same time. I often wished that I had loved ones with me to see what I was seeing. Every time I saw something that took my breath away, it was immediately followed by the thought, *I wish my family were here.*

My social circle at that time consisted of the wives of other bankers, whose roles were as much about love as they were about duty. And me, I was now stepping into my role as a Lehman wife. At the time, there were terms of engagement that came with being a "Lehman wife," which were that our husbands (or partners, as Ralph was then) worked for an astronomical number of hours each day making incredible salaries, and our job was to be supportive and keep the house in order. It wasn't anyone's fault; that's just the way it was. You didn't own your husband. The bank owned your husband. While it was tough not seeing Ralph as often as I might have liked, I adapted, because he did everything he could to make me happy, and even when we were apart we truly did love each other.

And then Ralph proposed, in the Ralphest way imaginable. I honestly can't remember if this was before Hong Kong or after, but I know it was before London and that it involved a trip to my parents'. One day, Ralph took a walk to the barn in our backyard with my father and asked him for my hand in marriage. After receiving the okay from Dad, Ralph took the car and journeyed to Philadelphia because a friend had told him about an exceptional treasure of a jewelry shop—the type of family-owned place where everything is done by hand. He picked out a stone, set it in a simple silver setting, and, in Great Barrington, he got on one knee and asked me to marry him. I of course said yes, and with that we started planning our wedding.

The first step was picking the venue, and that was easy. I wanted to get married at the Blantyre Castle in Lenox, Massachusetts. It was owned by Senator John and Jane Fitzpatrick, who also owned the Red Lion Inn in Stockbridge, where I had waitressed for all those years. Back then, if you got lucky you'd get chosen to serve at special events at the castle. I had been chosen, and it was during my time waitressing there, walking around with a tray, that my dream of getting married at Blantyre had formed.

This dream had always seemed completely inaccessible, especially since in order to have a wedding there, you had to rent the entire castle. At the time, it was very expensive, and though my parents had become financially secure by then, I was not about to ask them to pay for a very expensive wedding. But of course they wanted to pay for the wedding. That's tradition! To them, though, the idea of getting married at the Blantyre Castle was just unimaginable. And so, I had to figure out a way to get married at the castle while allowing my parents to be involved financially.

Well (surprise surprise), I figured out a way. Thankfully, the Fitzpatricks had always valued my work ethic and been kind to me. The senator had even written me a beautiful recommendation for college. When it came time to get married, I asked them for a favor. If I could get all the rooms filled with our friends and if my parents paid for the reception, could I possibly have the keys to the castle for a day? The senator and Jane graciously agreed, and I was over the moon.

It was a huge full-circle moment in my life to have my wedding reception at the Blantyre Castle, and beyond my wildest dreams. The wedding was in the fall of 1991. Ralph and I were twenty-seven years old. His Scottish friends wore kilts and sporrans and my bridesmaids wore Laura Ashley. Ralph and I got married at St. Peter's Church in Great Barrington, the same church where my grandparents and my parents had been married. The only difference was that this time, there was a bagpiper outside the doors of the chuch, announcing the big day to our small town. It was truly a magical wedding, and it marked the start of my new life.

After Ralph and I got married in October, we took an amazing three-week honeymoon through Thailand and Bali before returning to London. It was now official; I was married to a Scotsman and Britain was my home. Ralph could continue opening offices and making deals, and I could make us a home. London exceeded my expectations and I instantly fell in love with the city. People dressed up. People valued tradition. Everyone was *just so glamorous*, they dazzled effortlessly. They made the ordinary feel luxurious. London was like a white cashmere blanket that is used every day but never gets stained or pills.

I can remember one night in particular, when we went to a party hosted by one of Ralph's friends and his leggy, gorgeous Italian wife. Upon our arrival, the door was opened not by the wife, but by a door person. When it happened, I remember literally jumping a bit. "Oh." I was overwhelmed by the extravagance of it. And the Italian wife wasn't dressed in a basic A-line dress, but rather in a long satin number that made her look so elegant—but not pretentious. At one point she put on music and everyone started dancing, and the dress moved with her like water. All I could think about was, *Okay, Dorinda, you need to go home and burn all your A-line dresses.*

The real kicker was that in the center of their beautiful serving table was a gigantic sterling silver bowl filled with shrimp cocktail. When I was growing up, shrimp cocktail was the alpha and omega of foods. It was the thing on the menu you always looked at but were never allowed to order. To me, it was reserved for very special occasions and even then you'd be lucky if you got more than one or two. And there it was right before my eyes, a castle of shrimp cocktail. I couldn't believe it.

I whispered to Ralph, "I've never seen so much shrimp in my life."

Ralph hadn't seen that much shrimp in his life either. Since we'd both grown up in middle-class families, we were awed by this opulence together. The truth is that we were both kind of awkward in our life at first. We wore it like we were playing dress-up.

Our first real home was a gorgeous two-bedroom apartment in Eaton Place in Belgravia, right between Buckingham Palace and Sloane Square. The apartment was beautiful, with two bedrooms decorated in a traditional British style. The living room had Osborne & Little English-style floral curtains with tiebacks that draped over the French doors, which opened up to a view of Belgravia. We had velvet couches and a formal dining room. It was everything I had dreamed of, and now it was my home. It came with a key to Eaton Square, which was just across the street from our place, and I remember being unable to wrap my head around it. I thought, *What do you mean we have a key to a square? Also, what is a square?*

This square turned out to be a beautifully maintained common garden across the street from our apartment, surrounded by a black gate that served more as a symbol than a guarded perimeter. There was a lot of subtle pageantry in London and the square was sacred ground for it. Most of my friends in New York were still living post-college lifestyles, and I now had a key to Eaton Square? It was beyond what I could have imagined. The apartment came with a full kitchen and a proper dining room. And I got my first *real* set of china and glassware.

I was now officially a serious adult—a *very* serious adult. The funny thing was that I didn't really know how to be an adult at all, or at least not a posh kind of adult. Yes, I'd been exposed to wives who were the Olympians of glamour, but when it was my turn to run our home in London I did it like my mother. I tried to replicate the warm and cozy feeling of my childhood. Every morning, I would get up early with Ralph and make us breakfast and iron his shirts. It was like a love language that bonded us. We hired a housekeeper, but it didn't feel natural to me to let somebody else do all the household tasks, so we did them together. I felt like cooking and cleaning were essential parts of making a home and I wanted to take part.

I also wanted to fit in, and so I started shopping and dressing like a Londoner. Even though I wasn't a full adult at this time, I felt like I was "adulting" in my new clothes. I shopped at Harrods, Harvey Nichols, Joseph, and other upscale stores on Sloane Avenue, and over time I amassed a wardrobe that was sophisticated and chic. I came to look like an investment banker's wife. I learned from the women around me. The Chanel jackets they bought—I bought those, too. The handbags they carried—I carried those, too. For the first time ever I felt like a glamorous person. I would try on a pair of the most basic black pants you've ever seen, but when I looked at myself wearing them in the mirror at Selfridges it was like I was wearing an evening gown.

I couldn't work in London because I didn't have a visa, so along with shopping I would spend the day busying myself with errands. There was a separate shop for every item. I went to the fishmonger in Chelsea Square for fish and to the specialty cheese shop for cheese. Going to the bank back then was a full affair. You had to make an appointment to take money out of your account, and then you would go and sit at the bank, Coutts & Co, and explain to your banker that you needed to withdraw 200 pounds, and by the time you were done half the day was gone.

Making friends in America was so easy. You could meet a stranger at a bus stop and be their best friend three days later. But in London, it was different. People were much more guarded. So, before

I made any true friends, I got to know everybody in my neighborhood and all the employees at the places where I shopped. I became best friends with the guy who worked at the Floris counter at Peter Jones. I would wave to the fishmonger in Chelsea Square whenever I passed by, and the butcher at Partridges knew me by name. This, by the way, is still something I do today. I get to know my community, and I value my community.

The first real friend I made in London was a woman named Anne. One night, Ralph and I were out walking and he pointed to a house and said, "My boss lives there. He runs all of Lehman London." Since he knew what I was thinking, he added, "Do *not* go knocking on that door tomorrow."

Well, the very next day, can you guess what I did? I knocked on the door. I was curious and lonely and wanted to believe I could make a connection with another American expat. The fact that Anne lived in my neighborhood made it feel necessary. I wasn't going to walk by her house every day knowing a potential friend lived there!

Anne, immediately, was a breath of fresh air in my life. Like me, she was a little against the grain. When you put us next to the other Lehman wives, we didn't quite fit in. Anne felt isolated like I did, and we hit it off instantly. If you can believe it, Anne was actually the first person who ever gave Hannah a bath. And Hannah, even now, calls her Auntie Anne. Later, Anne and I both ended up back in New York, but I'll tell you more about that later.

Another important early friend of mine in London was Heather Kerzner, whom I met at a Junior League meeting. While scanning the room to see if I knew anyone or if there was anyone there I wanted to know, I caught sight of this wacky gorgeous woman in Kenzo pants who was carrying a straw bag with a broken handle. Heather and I fell in love immediately, and we've been friends for almost thirty years.

Things were going well. I didn't have a ton of friends, but I had a few, and I loved Ralph so much. The great thing about him was that he always saw me as an integral part of our partnership. We were equals and I had an important role to play in *our* success. Ralph never referred to it as *his* success, but always *our* success. Ralph would go to work, and I would take care of the home and the finances. Like my mother, I controlled the bank accounts. I reconciled the statements at the end of the month. If I can give you a piece of advice, it's this: Know where your money is going. If your partner is making the income, then track it. If you're making the income, then track it. If you want to be financially successful in any capacity, you need to understand where you're spending your money and how to manage it. I shopped a lot, but I didn't spend more than what we could afford.

Lehman not only got us an apartment but they also made sure we knew what to do with it. I went to etiquette classes at the British School of Etiquette. This was in the early nineties, post-Thatcher, when everything in London was very formal. The reason to go to the school was not only to learn how to set the table beautifully for Ralph's colleagues when they came over for dinner. It was also to get acclimated to the way things were done in London. As an American, I was totally unfamiliar.

The school included various classes that all focused on teaching us about the culture of Britain. I learned how to set the table and how to write a good thank-you card and a good invitation. I learned how to be a good hostess and a good guest and which fork and knife go where and how far apart they should be on a place mat. I literally learned how to use a ruler to measure the distance between the cutlery and the plate. The classes helped me understand the culture of my new country in a fuller way, and they helped me to feel like I belonged there. I loved how formal it was, and I still use what I learned to this day.

Entertaining became a big and very rewarding part of my life (as it still is), and I took my role as a dinner party host very seriously. I bought *The Silver Palate Cookbook*, which was considered quintessential back then, and it became my new bible. I would study it intensely and choose dishes based on how impressive they sounded. Chicken with a sweet white wine sauce and dried apricots? Yes. Spaghetti sauce made with champagne? Yes! After choosing which dishes to cook, I would write out my menus with vigor—at noon, because preparation is everything.

I know what you're thinking. It's old-fashioned and sort of sexist to assume that all women should care about how to set a dinner table, but that was part of the job that I'd signed up for and, quite frankly, learning how to host in my twenties served me well for all the years that came after. It's important to understand these things, not just for your husband but for yourself. Let's face it, when you're on a date or at a work dinner and someone is holding their fork and knife like a tennis racket and hitting their food around their plate like a ball it's a turnoff. Like, where's the modern-day video for how to hold your cutlery? Now there's a TikTok I would watch.

At first, I loved everything about my London life, but after the initial high wore off, I was lonely again. I had the wooden hangers and the fragranced candles and the Chanel, but what was the point if I had no one to talk to all day? In the beginning, I would cook Ralph elaborate dinners for when he came home from work, but then he was working later and later, so I stopped. Ralph got up at 5:30 in the morning and wouldn't come home until late.

When I'd envisioned spending my life with someone, I'd seen us hanging out and having fun and growing old together, which was turning out to be unrealistic. The reality of Ralph's intense job didn't allow for that, and I didn't feel comfortable complaining about it to my friends back home, who were still getting their nails done on Second Avenue and going to happy hour at Coconut Grill. Now that I had everything I'd ever wanted, I couldn't help but miss what I had left behind.

At the time, I didn't understand how hard it must have been on Ralph, who was twenty-seven years old with an enormous amount of responsibility on his shoulders. On Saturdays, I'd want him to get up and go out with me, but he was tired. My reactions to this weren't perfect, to be honest.

"I want you to be home more! I want to go out to dinner! I want to go out dancing at Annabel's!"

Ralph couldn't understand why I was complaining and his inability to fix the situation overwhelmed him, especially because

Ralph is a solution-oriented person. I didn't need a solution, because I was well aware that there wasn't one. I just wanted to talk about it, because that's how I process. I can't see what's going on until I externalize it. The clarity that comes with speaking my thoughts out loud often *is* the solution for me.

Ralph always suggested that I spend more time with the other Lehman wives, but I didn't ever feel like I fit in with them, and I didn't feel like I'd been fully invited into their circle yet either. When I would go to their houses for tea, I always felt like I was on the periphery of a group—like there was a room within a room that I couldn't see and wasn't supposed to see. It never really crossed my mind whether I even *wanted* to be their friend or not. Something about them not letting me in made me want to try harder, which created a lot of insecurity.

My world was transforming, and I was especially aware of that whenever I would return to the United States to visit my friends and see my family. It made me miss my old life even more.

I decided that part of the issue in London was our neighborhood. Belgravia was a very traditional, old-world place in London, a place where everyone took everything very seriously. It was the kind of place where you were never really sure if anyone liked you or not. It all felt like a job interview. And on top of that, it was not very lively or fun.

There are two types of people in this world: the people who love to dance and the people who don't love to dance. I wanted to find a place with people who loved to dance and didn't take themselves too seriously—and that place was not Belgravia.

Where would Ralph and I move to? I remembered the fabulous Italians who had thrown the party with the shrimp cocktail, and I decided that I was done with tea. I wanted shrimp. I wanted to live where the Italians lived.

So, we moved to the Boltons, where I found the most beautiful apartment, which I still think about to this day. The neighborhood was lively, filled with young parents and their children. Every room in the new apartment seemed to come with a bonus. It had two massive double doors that opened up to a garden. We had a beautiful dining room that was attached to a more formal sitting room. I loved it.

I immediately bonded with our upstairs neighbor, Mrs. Holland, who was a descendant of the famously gay and controversial poet Lord Alfred Douglas. She was very old and possibly the most eccentric person I've ever met. I love eccentric people, in case you haven't put that together yet. When we moved in, she came downstairs and said, "I would like you to join me for tea on the first Wednesday of every month."

Of course I agreed. I was still looking for friends. In fact, I'd even joined the Junior League and then the Knightsbridge Women's Club looking for friends, but those people weren't really my people. I wanted to make friends with Londoners—friends who weren't expats and who weren't, therefore, going to leave in a few years for their next corporate transfer. I wanted to become a sort of local myself. (Remember Ralph was a British citizen, so I thought we were never leaving.)

I quit both clubs shortly after I joined them. I was much happier

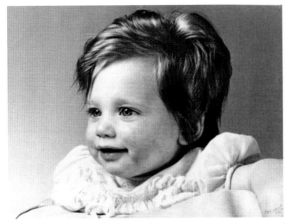

My baby picture (1965)

When Mom brought Melinda
home from the hospital
(1966)

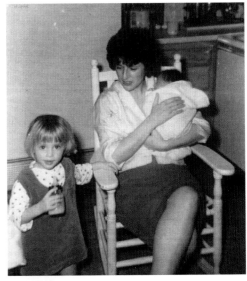

My First Communion
with Grandma
Magadini, Grandma
Cinkala, and family
(St. Peter's Church,
Great Barrington,
MA, 1974)

Melinda and me riding bikes in Great Barrington, MA (1975)

Me after moving to NYC in 1989, going to the Puck Building with Susan McCarthy

Wedding photo with Ralph Lynch (St. Peter's Church, Great Barrington, MA, 1991)
Keith Torrie

With bridesmaid June Marshall at my wedding to Ralph Lynch (St. Peter's Church, Great Barrington, MA, 1991) *Keith Torrie*

Wedding photo with Ralph Lynch (Blantyre, Lenox, MA, 1991)
Keith Torrie

Pregnant with Hannah
(London, 1993)

Hours after I gave birth
to Hannah Lynch
(Portland Hospital, London,
December 26, 1993)

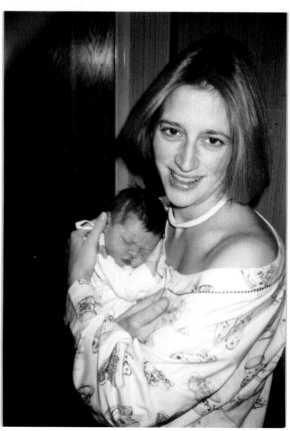

Hannah meeting Santa at
Harrods (London, 1994)
Ralph Lynch

Me and Hannah
(Nice, France, 1994)

Hannah's baptism, with her godfather, John Cinkala, her godmother, Zoe Lynch, and Ralph Lynch (St. Peter's Church, Great Barrington, MA, 1994)

At Hannah's baptism, with June Marshall and Deborah Rausch (1994)

Summertime with Hannah in Hyannisport, MA (1996)

Hannah learning to ski in Verbier, Switzerland (winter 1998)

My wedding to Richard, with my mom and Hannah (October 2005)
Tanya Tribble

My wedding to
Richard, with
Hannah, and Paige
and Aidan Medley
(October 2005)
Tanya Tribble

At our wedding reception at The Grill at the Seagram Building (New York City, October 2005)
Tanya Tribble

Dancing with my father at my wedding at The Grill at the Seagram Building (October 2005)
Tanya Tribble

Richard and me with Hillary Clinton at a fundraiser for her at our townhouse (2008)
Tanya Tribble

With Richard and Hannah on our Hinckley boat, *Leopardo* (Hyannisport, MA, 2009)

With my mother—my rock—one year after Richard died (2012)

Blue Stone Manor
Copyright Mick Hales

Master bedroom
at Blue Stone
Manor. Interiors
by Marshall
Watson
Interiors.
*Copyright Mick
Hales*

Peacock-blue
living room
at Blue Stone
Manor. Interiors
by Marshall
Watson Interiors.
Copyright Mick Hales

John Mahdessian and me
(June 2015)

Christmas card (New York City, 2015)

Nutcracker Gate
on *RHONY*
Season 10 (2017)

LEFT: Season 10 reunion, with Carole Radziwill (2018)
RIGHT: Season 11 reunion, with Sonja Morgan and Ramona Singer (2019)

Watch What Happens Live, "The Night of 31 Doorbells" (Los Angeles, April 2018) *Whitney Cinkala*

With Mom and Dad at Blue
Stone Manor (2019)
Myrna Suárez, Twin B Photography

Bravo green screen photo
shoot with my friend
and makeup artist Luke
Henderson (2019)

Hosting *Make It Nice*
on Sirius XM (New
York City, 2019)

WWHL with friends Mona Andrikian, James Palazza, and Patrick Michael (July 2019)

My Season 11 reunion look, in a Naeem Khan dress (2019)

Christmas with Hannah at Blue Stone Manor (2020)

Christmas at Blue Stone Manor (2020)

Hannah and me at Dorado Beach, Puerto Rico (2021)

going upstairs to hang out with Mrs. Holland, who would tell me the most fantastic stories of London in the old days. She lived in a beautiful apartment that was a mess of days gone by, with mosslike film growing in the bathtub and stacks of old London *Times* newspapers on the table. Her mantel was covered in crested invitations to events that had passed. I adored Mrs. Holland. On top of her head she always wore the tightest chignon. She was so much more interesting than the too-perfect cookie-cutter wives. A façade of perfection, at the end of the day, is just kind of boring.

I got to know all the vendors of the shops I liked in the Boltons and became a repeat customer. Eventually, the vendors became my friends, and after I had friends in the neighborhood it felt like *my* neighborhood. I continued to spend my days shopping and planning elaborate dinner parties and seeing the new friends I had made. I was going to church every week. In a nutshell, I was really beginning to carve out a life for myself in London.

I still missed working, though, and at some point I decided I should start teaching aerobics again. When I found out what a council flat was, I knew it would be the ideal venue. Council flats are basically subsidized housing communities full of working-class people. I found one in Wandsworth, just outside London, with a huge common space you could rent for 25 pounds an hour.

I rented the common space and put up a sign.

Aerobics! 3 pounds! 5 p.m. Tuesday!

Then, at 5:00 p.m. on Tuesday, I showed up in my spandex with my Dyna-Bands and my boom box ready to go. The class was wildly successful. The women in Wandsworth had never seen anything like it. Back then, everything happened in America first and took three to five years to cross the pond, so aerobics wasn't big in the UK yet, and it was especially foreign to this group of people.

I would give them a break halfway through the hour because they weren't very good, and everybody would light up a cigarette. I thought it was hilarious. I'd yell, "Smoke break's over!" and we'd move on to the second half. The husbands would be sitting on the sides drinking lager and cheering their wives on. I'm not sure if anyone in Wandsworth was serious about aerobics, but I know they loved my music.

Afterwards, I'd go over to their houses for tea and meet their kids. Even though London was only eight miles away, it might as well have been another world. This was definitely a stark contrast to my London life with Ralph, but I felt comfortable there. I loved it, and, as you know by now, I loved making my own money. I'd return home with bags filled with coins and then I'd go deposit them at my bank.

It was just after we moved to the Boltons that Ralph and I decided to start trying for a baby. One month after we made this decision, I went to New York for the opening of the Royalton Hotel, where I drank a ton of champagne. I threw up during the entire flight back home, thinking it was the worst hangover I'd ever had in my life. I just felt terrible. Then it dawned on me that I might be pregnant.

And I was right.

Ralph couldn't believe it. "What? We just started trying."

Pregnant now, I continued teaching aerobics in Wandsworth.

Often, when I would show up, there was a guy waiting for me in the parking lot, a local man in his early thirties who always seemed excited to see me and happy to help me bring my Dyna-Bands and my boom box into the hall before class. We would chat a little bit. I don't remember anything we said to each other, and I had no idea who he was. I appreciated his kindness, but he kind of creeped me out. To be honest, he *super* creeped me out. Why was he always there waiting for me? It seemed like he definitely knew my schedule. I didn't want to be alone with him, so I'd arrive just before the class started. After he helped me with my gear, he'd just sit on the sidelines in the hall and watch the class. It was weird. But not weird enough to do anything about it.

Then, one evening during class, Scotland Yard showed up and arrested him. Why? Because he was the Wandsworth Killer! The Wandsworth Killer was all over the news at the time, but I never made the connection. It seemed too crazy. The police told me they thought he might have been stalking me.

Ralph and I quickly put the kibosh on the aerobics thing after that—not only because I'd possibly almost been murdered but also because I was getting as big as a house and more uncomfortable each day.

Some women get pregnant elegantly. They're still wearing their jeans in the third trimester. And their bikinis. They look flawless. They're posing naked for black-and-white portraits. Their baby bumps are sexy. They go water-skiing like it's no big deal.

This was the type of pregnant woman I wanted to be, but I was the opposite. I got huge. My feet swelled. I was miserable. After reading *What to Expect When You're Expecting*, I thought I was only going to have morning sickness for three months. Well, mine lasted into my fifth month. I didn't know what to wear, and there weren't many maternity stores in London then, because fabulous Europeans got cute-pregnant, not size-of-a house pregnant. It got to the point that my ob-gyn, Mr Gillard (baby doctors in Britain go by "Mr," not "Dr"), stopped weighing me, and when I asked why he responded that the baby had had enough food!

Can you imagine? But was I going to stop eating? Absolutely not. I went on eating everything in sight until the bitter end. I especially loved savory. Breakfast often consisted of cold Heinz baked beans on a baked potato. I loved cottage cheese and ramen noodles. I gained sixty-two pounds altogether. The average weight gain for a pregnant woman is about twenty-five to thirty-five pounds, just so you know.

On Boxing Day, which is a huge holiday in Britain the day after Christmas, when most people don't go to work, Ralph went off to work. "If you're having the baby, call me," he said.

Well, I figured I would rather go to a party I was invited to than sit at home alone, so that's what I did. So there I was at my friend's luncheon, having a good time—until heartburn hit. It was the most intense heartburn I'd ever felt. My stomach was tightening up. I excused myself and went home, and that's when I realized I was having contractions.

I called Ralph. "I think I'm having a baby."

"Are you sure?" he asked.

"I'm over nine months pregnant. Yes, I'm sure!" They didn't do inductions back then, so Hannah had been overcooking in the oven.

Ralph said he'd meet me at the hospital. I hobbled out of the apartment and got into a black taxi. The taxi driver was so worried about me having a baby on the way there that he told me to lie down. I did what he said. I lay on the floor of a cab on my way to the Portland Hospital in Mayfair, which, at the time, was where all the "it" women of London went to give birth. It was also known for its specialization in pediatric intensive care. Little did I know how important this would become a few months later when my newborn, Hannah, needed to go back. All I knew was that on December 26, 1993, my best friend was born. I say this to Hannah every year.

To my daughter, Hannah:
I fell in love with you as a little seed,
I cherished you as a child,
and I am in awe of you as an adult.

Chapter Five

AND THEN SHE LOOKED AT ME

In the hours before Hannah's birth, I was totally unaware of how greatly she would impact my life. I thought I was going to give birth, have some lobster and champagne, then go home, hire a nanny, and continue my regular life with a new baby. The anticipation was not of Hannah, but of what Hannah would add to my life. She would be the punctuation mark at the end of a perfect sentence that I had written. As far as I was concerned, she was going to come out of the womb in a Bonpoint outfit.

But as I began to push, the experience started to change me. It was as though a piece of my soul was being drawn out of my body. They lifted her up, and I couldn't help but feel that even though she was no longer inside me, there was an invisible cord attaching us that couldn't be cut. They placed her head on my chest, and it landed beneath my shoulder like a puzzle piece. In an instant, her little body had pushed me to the deepest depths of myself and uncovered a love so profound that to call it love would be like describing pasta as salad. The feeling was big enough to upend the checklist I had centered my life around. On some level, that frightened me.

And then she looked at me. She looked at me with eyes that held the history of everything and the potential of everything, full of familiarity and expectancy. Parting her lips, she exhaled on my chin. Her breath smelled like a dream I had never thought to dream. Her face was like a memory that got lost in time, a story that you need someone to retell in order to remember. *I know you. You know me. We know each other. You're Hannah.*

There was also an overwhelming sense of power that came over me in that moment. Like, the first time someone told me the story about the woman who lifted a two-ton car to save her baby, it had kind of felt like a joke to me. Now I suddenly got it. I could lift a car for Hannah. There was nothing I wouldn't do for this nine-pound person. If I had thrown my arms up in that moment, wings would have literally sprung from them like in those Egyptian pictures of Isis. I might have made Hannah, but she had also made *me*.

As I held Hannah for the first time, I thought of my mother. I missed her more than ever, and my connection to her deepened. It felt like I had become a link in a long chain of women that stretched back to my mother and my grandmother and now through to Hannah. My grandmother died shortly after Hannah's birth, and looking back, there was something kind of mystical about the timing. It was almost as though Hannah's arrival had signaled to my grandmother that she could let go.

Ralph was beside himself in love. A couple of minutes into doing "skin to skin" (when they have the baby lie on the woman's chest), I looked over at Ralph, who was undoing the top buttons of his collared shirt, in an open declaration that he would also be doing skin to skin, even though there was no real precedent for fathers doing that. In many ways, Ralph and I had already begun to grow apart, but there was something about Hannah's birth that trivialized any worry I had had about our marriage. We just loved her so much. Hannah's presence was a fertilizer that made love grow wherever she was. Our love for Hannah bonded us forever, and it's the reason why we were truly able to raise her together.

We took her home, and even though I was often tired, it was absolute heaven. I can remember actually missing Hannah when she would go to sleep. She was an easy baby, so long as I didn't stray too far. Whenever I left the room she would lose it, which meant we were pretty much together all the time.

One day when Hannah was a few months old, I invited a couple of my friends over to see the baby. I put Hannah in a bouncer right by my chair and as usual bounced her gently to sleep, with her staring at me as I did it. About thirty minutes later, I was putting the kettle on to make some tea when one of my friends screamed! I knew immediately that something had happened to Hannah. My heart sank. In a millisecond, fear swallowed me whole. When I turned to look, her skin was blue and her tongue was sticking out of her mouth. I went to pick her up. She'd stopped breathing. I started frantically patting her back, repeating over and over, "Hannah. . . .

Come on, Hannah. . . . Hannah, please. . . . Hannah! Hannah!" She opened her lips and started to cry. Then I started to cry. I grabbed a blanket and we rushed to the hospital. I called Ralph in hysterics and soon after he arrived dripping with sweat because he'd run half the way to beat traffic.

They put a little oxygen mask on Hannah. According to the nurses, everything was fine. She was breathing normally and her heart rate was normal. Ralph and I were relieved, but we also knew there was something they weren't telling us, and we were right. When the doctor came in, he said in the most matter-of-fact way, "We suspect it's apnea."

The doctor explained that apnea was a sleep disorder where you go into such a deep sleep that you stop breathing and that he was going to perform a test to confirm his diagnosis. He took Hannah and put her on this leathery table with crunchy paper that just looked so unbearably cold and uncozy to me. She was screaming hysterically. The combination of the crunchy sound and the sound of her wailing tortured me. But I held back, because I trusted it was the right thing to do.

Then two nurses came in. "Hold her down," one said.

Apparently, they had to hold her down so they could pour water down her throat to see if she could catch her breath in distress.

I freaked out. "Nope! No way, no how, no. No, that is too aggressive and I'm not having it; she's too little!"

"Mr. Lynch, please get control of your wife."

I can't even remember what happened after that, because I pretty much blacked out. Worse, I redded out. I saw red. I picked Hannah up and placed her on the top of my thigh so she could sit up straight and catch her breath. We put the oxygen mask back on her when she'd calmed down and Ralph eventually took her to his chest, walking around the room to comfort her. I walked behind them to make sure the mask didn't get tangled and watched Hannah's little face droop on Ralph's shoulder as she fell asleep.

"I literally won't make it, Ralph." I didn't need to say it for Ralph to understand what I meant: *If she dies, I won't make it.*

At this point, it was the middle of the night, so we waited a couple hours in the hospital in case she stopped breathing again, and then we went straight to a specialist.

The pediatric hospital we went to was just outside London. It was the grayest place I had ever seen, and going there was like entering a universe that had never known color. But it was the best, and it was where Hannah needed to be. After seeing the doctor, we were informed that Hannah would have to stay the night for observation. The nurse walked us down the hall to a glass window full of flat-bottom cribs with high bars lined up in neat rows. Like a prison.

I handed Hannah off and asked where the parents slept.

"Oh no, Mrs. Lynch," the nurse responded. "Mummies and daddies go home for the evening and can return at seven a.m."

As you can imagine, that one went over like a lead balloon. Ralph went home and I decided to get in the crib with Hannah. I coiled my body around her like a snake with her eggs. The truth is, I probably did it as much for me as I did it for her. In the previous eight hours I had heard the acronym "SIDS" (Sudden Infant Death Syndrome) more times than any new mother ever should, and just hearing it was enough to make me believe it could happen. What if I left and this was it? What if she went into a seizure and died alone? What if someone kidnapped her? I was so scared.

The next day they put Hannah on a breathing monitor and sent her home. It was a nightmare. Leaving her to go to work was torture for Ralph. Watching her suffer was torture for me. Every four hours I would have to take off the EKG wires and replace them with new ones. I stopped sleeping. The fear I had in the hospital stayed with me always. I would lie in bed while she slept and think, *What if I go to sleep and this is the last time I ever see her?* Luckily, the monitor had an alarm, but to be honest, it didn't really help. Ralph's parents and grandparents lived in Scotland and came down to assist, which was great, but it wasn't until my mother arrived that I really got a good night's sleep. I remember my mother came to London on a Friday and for the first time I handed Hannah off. After that, I slept and slept and slept, knowing Hannah was safe and looked after.

After a couple months, they told me Hannah no longer had to wear her breathing monitor, which floored me. It was like they had randomly picked a date on a calendar to take it off. It freaked me out to be honest. Hannah went from being my biggest worry to being my joy and purpose. She filled up every void that had been in my life. I didn't feel lonely anymore because I had this little pal to take care of whom I just adored.

Hannah wasn't a difficult baby, so long as certain conditions were met. The second too many people came into the house, she would go nuts. She was a constant observer and always looked like she was in a deep state of thought. She had this stare that made you feel like she really *saw* things and internalized them. When the world got too big for Hannah she couldn't handle it and would have a fit.

At six o'clock in the morning, I'd hear Hannah's noises on the baby monitor. She didn't cry. She sounded more like a monster: "Ra ra ra." I'd go into her room and she'd be sitting in the corner of her crib looking at me with her huge eyes. Her eyes would light up like she couldn't believe I had shown up again. It was the best feeling in the world. This became a double-edged sword, though, because she would get herself in a panic every time I left her alone. I couldn't let her get too hysterical because I was always afraid about her losing her breath. It was too much at times. I couldn't even take a bath anymore. I would literally have to stick her bouncy in the bathroom with me and she would wave at me the whole time.

Motherhood was the biggest commitment I had ever made, and it wasn't always easy. At times it felt monotonous and isolating. Every day was the same thing, and it was difficult with Ralph being at work so often. Even though I loved her so much, I needed to see an end to our long days together, so I was very strict about Hannah's sleeping schedule. Bedtime was at 6:30 p.m. no matter what. Even if I was in the middle of winning the lottery, I would put her to bed at 6:30. Having that to look forward to kept me sane.

Friends became an extremely important part of my life in London. One was Caroline. Every day, I would put Hannah in her pram and take a walk to the local church. I thought the fresh air would be good for her and that the prayers and lit candles would be good for us both. I had seen Caroline a couple times before, but it wasn't until I happened upon her son's baptism that we connected. She was the most elegant person I had ever seen. She had big blue eyes, blond hair, and was incredibly soft-spoken. I desperately needed friends and she probably felt bad for me on some level after seeing Hannah in her oxygen mask, so we ended up exchanging information.

Soon after, I received a letter at my door: *Dear Dorinda, I was wondering if you're available for tea at 4 p.m. on February 16th—* which, by the way, was almost a month away at the time. She had introduced herself as Caroline, but the name on the card was something different. *Lady MacTaggart.* It felt like I had just been informed that the white horse I had met was in fact a unicorn. I couldn't just call her back to RSVP; the protocol in London was totally different. Ralph informed me that the correct thing to do was to have stationery made and return the letter. So, that's exactly what I did. Caroline was formal and somewhat guarded, but she was cheeky and I liked that. It was a relationship that I knew would take time to cultivate, but I enjoyed her company and she had a son who was Hannah's age. Over time, the water in the moat between us drained. She went from being the Lady down the street to being my girlfriend, and she still is to this day.

Having Hannah became a way for me to make friends with other mothers. My life became play dates, birthday parties, and suppers with other moms. I started going away for long weekends at their country houses, and Ralph didn't want to go because he felt awkward. He didn't know my new friends, and they didn't really know him either. They came to know me independently, as a woman named Dorinda with a husband named Ralph. My friend group in London was like family to me. It consisted of a real mix of people: American bankers, British artists and designers, and other mothers. Mothers raised their kids as a community in England. We did everything together, and it was great because it made up for the space that Ralph left by being at work all the time.

When Hannah was about a year old, we moved neighborhoods, from the Boltons to the Little Boltons because it was finally time to get a more family-friendly home. The Little Boltons had a huge garden, a big kitchen, a more formal dining and sitting area, and a quaint red front door.

About once a month, Ralph and I would go to Scotland. His family lived in a small town just outside Glasgow where the weather, like in the rest of Scotland, was gloomy. They didn't seem to mind, though. The house was often kept at a low temperature, but they were such hearty people that they barely noticed. When we'd bring Hannah up, it would light up their world. I came to look forward to my stays in Scotland. I loved that Hannah had an extended family. The Scots were so different from the Londoners I knew—more colorful and quirky and, quite frankly, more accepting in a lot of ways. I enjoyed the great mince dinners, and the visits to Great-Gran's House for Jell-O and Hobnobs. An American in Scotland was a welcomed oddity.

It was during my time in Scotland that I started my first business. When we first began going there, it was always so chilly that I was in constant search of the perfect sweater. There were two options if you wanted a cashmere sweater. Cheap, thick, and shapeless or expensive, thin, and impractical. Why did everything have to be a twin set or a pullover? Why were the arms so big? Why were the cuts so unflattering?

I started using my weekends to visit Scottish cashmere factories with my friend Belinda Robertson. I was mesmerized by the manufacturing process. I watched a sweater being put together like it was an episode of *Law & Order*. I still love watching how things are made. On some level, the behind-the-scenes action has always been more interesting to me than what's onstage.

The Scottish factories were actually old millhouses where the same families had worked for generations. They were spotlessly clean and totally enchanting. After perusing with Belinda, I bought a bunch of cashmere garments and started making my own prototypes. I'd take a sweater, for example, and tailor it in a new way, a way that made it look sexier and more fun. I created cardigans with loose arms, and big chunky turtlenecks that you could wear with riding pants and boots to replace the horrendous dark green jackets with the corduroy collars that everyone wore. I added elements for extra flair to everyday pieces. I made robes with huge satin cuffs and thick sashes. I made baby blankets with fun trim and giant throw blankets in every color imaginable. I was making what I wanted to wear, which was what I assumed other women my age would want to wear, too. And thankfully, they did.

I knew I was onto something with designing the sexier cuts, but the details were trickier. Different women would want different color combinations and different fabric embellishments. I also knew that everyone back then wanted to be a designer. With all this in mind, I came up with a business model—one that would incorporate the desires of cashmere-loving women. I would start by presenting the customer with a basic piece, like a cardigan, for example, in a variety of styles and base colors. The customer could choose her color, her own style, and her own buttons. She could make all the buttons the same or she could go nuts and choose a bunch of different buttons for the same cardigan. Then she'd choose the trim. Did she want velvet? Fur? No trim? I would write all of her choices down on an order form and send it away. Then, six weeks later, a box would arrive at her house. My customers loved having a hand in what they made, and I enjoyed helping them bring their vision to life.

I loved what I did and selling it was easy. Instead of opening a shop, I'd host these fabulous tea parties at our house in the Little Boltons. The concept worked. The process was creative and fun. And the other great thing about this business model was that I never needed to carry stock. Everything was made to order. The pieces sold themselves. All I needed was for my clients to wear them so that their friends would ask, "Where did you get that?" Marketing was like a chain reaction or like a bouncing ball, going from one woman to another to another. Princess Diana became one of my clients because we had friends in common, and I thought this was amazing. The whole thing was amazing. I was making my own money and becoming known for what I created rather than whose wife I was. I was being introduced at parties as Dorinda, the woman with the clothing company. I chose a simple name for the brand. DCL Cashmere. And I have to say, the classic logo I came up with was *on point*.

I felt like I'd been given the keys to the kingdom that was my own, and I was never giving them back. The girl who'd woken up early in the morning to iron her husband's shirts was now long gone. I had taken a step out into the world, and I loved it. Having Hannah had given me purpose, and in a strange, paradoxical way it inspired me to become more independent and social. I adored London, and I also adored having a daughter who spoke to me in a British accent and called me Mummy. I had a housekeeper, Marietta, who helped take care of Hannah, but I was a very hands-on mom. Or mummy.

Over time, it became clear that Ralph and I were living different lives. I loved being with my friends, who now knew more about my everyday life than my husband did. Ralph was still working fifteen hours a day, and when he got home he didn't have the energy to go out dancing at Annabel's. He just wanted to be home with Hannah. Looking back, I don't really blame him. He just wanted to enjoy his daughter and rest.

I think before endings happen we can feel them coming on some level. We might not acknowledge them right away, but we can feel them. It was like that with Ralph. There was the sense of an ending that loomed over everything. We loved each other, but that wasn't enough. We stayed together for as long as we believed we could change each other. But the truth was we couldn't. I wanted Ralph to become someone who wasn't Ralph, and he wanted me to become someone who wasn't me. Loving someone isn't enough in a marriage. We loved each other, but in the end, we were too different.

One night, we had a literal ships-in-the-night moment. I was going out as he was coming home from work. We passed by each other in the long hallway—and got into a fight.

"You're going out again?"

"Well, why not?"

Suddenly we were screaming. Ralph and I never fought, but this was a big one. Hannah was crying her eyes out. And it just hit us. This was not working anymore. Something had to change.

It wasn't a bad breakup. It was the opposite—incredibly amicable. Ralph and I didn't hate each other. We just didn't have compatible lives anymore. The thing we had in common was Hannah, but it wasn't right to stay married for a child.

I might have stayed with Ralph if he'd wanted to have more kids, but he didn't. He barely had enough time to spend with Hannah as it was, and this was something that made him feel terribly guilty. I still wanted to have more children, and at that point I thought it would be easy. I'd just divorce Ralph and meet someone else and have more kids with the new husband.

Little did I know that it wouldn't be that easy. After the protective umbrella of marriage was taken away, what did I have? I no longer had the security of a husband. And this meant, unfortunately, that I was not considered in the same way—by some people anyway.

I mentioned earlier that Londoners plan events months in advance. Well, before Ralph and I made the decision to separate I'd RSVP'd to a dinner party with the idea that Ralph would come with me. The friend who'd invited me heard about the separation and called and said, "I suppose you won't be coming now."

"What? No, I'll still come."

"Oh, darling," she said pityingly. "It's evens, not odds."

So, there you had it. In certain circles, I was a woman scorned— or at least a dinner party guest rejected. The separation was slow. Eventually, Ralph moved into another place and I stayed in our home in the Little Boltons. No matter what, I knew I'd be staying in London long enough for Hannah to finish the school year, but after that I thought it might be time to leave. She was seven years old. I couldn't live in our giant house forever, and even though I had friends who were like family, I also had my real family back in America. For years I had longed for home but could do without it. After separating from Ralph, I suddenly *needed* to go home. I felt that if I stayed in London any longer my daughter would be decidedly British and we would be staying for the rest of our lives.

So I kind of made the decision that we were going home. Home is where I go to lick my wounds after every big change in my life. I go out into the world, I hit rough waters, and then I go back home to be comforted. I sit at my childhood dining room table and my mom fixes me a tuna fish sandwich and tells me it's going to be okay, and it feels, as it's felt so many times before, like my parents' house is the sun and everything else is the planets that revolve around it.

I sold the cashmere company and moving back to America became my main focus. When summer hit, I packed up the house. I said good-bye to all the friends I hadn't known existed nine years before. I reflected on how much I'd changed since arriving in London, all bushy-tailed and bright-eyed, in awe over that giant bowl of shrimp at the party I went to early on. And then Hannah and I left.

Looking back, there's a part of me that feels a little guilty because I didn't consult Ralph as much as I should have before I left. Lucky for me, very soon after we moved, Ralph followed us. It was in New York where he met his now-wife, whom he adores. (So if you're reading this, Ralph, *you're welcome.*)

I rented a place in Hyannisport that summer, as I'd been doing for years. Even though Hannah and I had often gone there without Ralph because he had to work, being on the beach that summer felt strange. I was getting accustomed to my new status. I was no longer married. I was separated. I was no longer returning home to London. Home was America again. It was Massachusetts for the summer, and then it was back to good old New York.

Hannah was accepted at Sacred Heart, a Catholic school on the Upper East Side. I wanted her to have religion in her life, and reconnecting to the church in New York was important for me, too. I'd be lying if I didn't tell you that I felt a lot of shame about getting separated. I was the first woman in our family to do it. I felt embarrassed. The great thing about New York is that it's full of divorced women, which made me feel less alone.

We found an apartment three blocks from the school—or really, my friend Anne found it for us. Like me, Anne had recently split from her husband and returned to New York as a single mother, so we had a lot in common. The place she found us was two buildings down from hers, so it was easy to spend a lot of time together. We both had young children. We went to each other's apartments almost every day. We had the support of each other and the safety of the Upper East Side, which is a great place to raise children. What I remember most about my time living next to Anne is that we were all always laughing and eating. Hannah adored Anne and her kids, and so did I. Anne and I had always leaned on each other back in London, and it felt like we were taking on the world together in New York.

The transition was as easy as it could have been, but that still didn't mean it was easy. I didn't realize how much I had changed until I got back to New York. I didn't realize how British I'd become! I'd left as a struggling person working in the Garment District and come back as a single mom. The ages of twenty-five to thirty-four are formative years. You're defining yourself more specifically and deciding how you want to live. Well, I had apparently defined myself as more of a Brit than I'd imagined. I thought I still understood America because I visited often, but when I moved back I realized that I didn't understand America anymore at all.

The way children were raised was different. The way you went to parties was different. In England, when you're invited to a child's birthday party it's really more of an event for the mothers. Everybody dresses up. The mothers socialize and eat lovely food while the kids play fun games.

Soon after we arrived back in New York, Hannah was invited to a birthday party. I got her all dressed up in an Anthea Moore dress, with red tights and red patent-leather shoes and a headband. I dressed myself just as nicely. We bought a lovely birthday present and followed the instructions to the party—which turned out to be at the top of a building in a gym area. None of the mothers were there. There were only nannies. And the children were out of control, running around like crazy people. Hannah was horrified. A pizza got delivered and placed on a fold-out table, and the kids went nuts, diving at this pizza. I looked over and there was Hannah standing on the sidelines with her arms crossed. I asked her what was wrong, and she said, "I'm waiting for the cutlery, Momma!" But there was no cutlery. By the time she got to the pizza it was like a massacre had befallen it. We went home and I made her pizza pockets. She was thrilled and ate them with a fork and knife.

Ralph ended up getting a job at Credit Suisse and an apartment in the neighborhood. We were relaxed about how we split parenting duties. Ralph had a key to my apartment, and I had a key to his. Hannah would spend the nights with him on weekends, and if he didn't have time to shop for her favorite foods then I would buy them and stock his fridge so their weekend meals would be ready. We were in no rush to get technically divorced, and in fact, I wouldn't divorce Ralph until six years later, in 2005, when I decided to marry Richard.

Even though Ralph and I weren't together, our lives were very intertwined, and they still are, although it's different now. Ralph and his wife are like extended family to me. We're all very close. Back when Hannah was young, Ralph generously continued to support us financially and I devoted myself to motherhood. I picked Hannah up every day at school and cooked her dinner every night, and Ralph joined us when he could. Hannah's young life was structured, just as mine had been. A routine creates safety, and this is especially important in moments of transition.

In London I'd been a mother who balanced child-rearing duties with late nights dancing and socializing, but when we got back to New York I became a tame, stay-at-home mom, and a protective one. I didn't let Hannah sleep over at other kids' houses. I had them all come to ours. I probably had the smallest apartment out of all of Hannah's friends, but it didn't matter. I bought the kids sleeping bags. They were happy. And I could keep an eye on Hannah. I didn't want her heading in the wrong direction.

There were many good things about moving back to America, and one of them was that Hannah got to see my parents more often. We'd drive to Massachusetts on the weekends and I'd watch my mother teach Hannah how to cook, just as she'd done with me. My mother became, again, my rock. Everything that I loved about my childhood my parents were now giving to my daughter. It was grounding to watch them together, and I knew that I'd made the right decision by moving home.

Eventually, I started dating, but Hannah always remained my primary focus. I made the conscious decision that she would never see a man in our apartment. If I was dating someone who wanted to meet my daughter, my answer to that was, "Don't worry about it." I only wanted Hannah to meet boyfriends I was very serious about, ones who I thought could be husband material. The truth was that I really wanted to be married again and I still wanted more kids. Well, things clearly did not go according to my plan. I didn't like it at the time, but now I can see that everything unfolded as it was meant to.

I spent a few years dating men who weren't meant to become my next husband. Some of them were just plain wrong for me. Some of them were almost right, but not quite. I dated a man named Daniel for about three years, which was long enough to introduce him to Hannah. He loved Hannah and Hannah loved him. I still put Hannah first, though. If we went on vacation, Daniel would sleep in one room and Hannah and I would sleep in another. He never slept over at our apartment. And he was okay with that, because he was very close with his family, too.

On paper, Daniel was wonderful. In person, he was wonderful. But there was one problem. He didn't want to get married. I always got the sense he was waiting for someone better. After we broke up, I gave up on dating. It was just too hard as a single mother. I wasn't willing to put the effort into it anymore. Dating is time-consuming! You have to go to dinner and drinks five million times, and then you're probably going to find out the guy you're dating isn't right for you anyway. I not only decided to stop dating, I also decided that I needed to lower my expectations. I would probably never be married again, and maybe I didn't want to be either. What was the point? I liked my life with Hannah. Why change it?

Instead of looking for men, I started looking for a job. It was time to get back to work. But what was I going to do? I'd done sales; I'd done the fashion jobs; I'd done the cashmere company. I didn't want to go back to any of those—but I could see myself selling again, because I was so good at it. I also needed a flexible schedule. Even though Hannah was a a little older by then, I still wanted to pick her up from school every day and be involved in her life.

So, I became a real estate agent. One of my dearest friends, Sarah, and I decided to go work for a boutique firm. It was called Mercedes Burke and it was owned by a hip lesbian couple. Sarah had also moved from London, and we used our own experience with relocating from London to New York and turned it into a sort of niche market. We knew which neighborhoods British people would like and in what kinds of places. We had a lot of London-esque town houses and well-appointed apartments listed close to the park.

Sarah was a very close friend, so we were more than happy to cover for each other when one of us was on mom duty. The mutual support made it easy, and I genuinely enjoyed the job. I got to meet great people and go into their houses, which was fascinating. How people design their homes says so much about their personalities. You might think that you understand who a person is, but when you go into their house you often learn something new. If someone has wacky decor, you assume they must be quite colorful. If the decor is simple and white, you assume the person must be more Zen than you'd originally imagined. On Park Avenue, you might not expect a lot of hoarders, but this is wrong. There are a lot of hoarders on Park Avenue. People are full of surprises!

About two years into my life as a real estate agent, in 2003, I got a cold call from a woman named Karima. She was calling on behalf of her boss, Richard Medley, who was interested in buying a piece of property and wanted to set up some showings.

The first time I met Richard Medley, he was in his fifties, handsome, elegant, bald, and eccentric, but in a quiet way. He didn't say very much, but what he said landed. Richard was a person who either did things or didn't do them. Nothing was ever casual with Richard. He was all in or all out. He never chuckled. When he laughed, he *really* laughed, and his laughter could make me laugh at things I didn't even find funny. I thought he was generous and kind and obviously genius-level smart. I wasn't hugely impressed with the way that he dressed, if I'm being totally honest. I remember noticing some chest hairs popping out of the top of his shirt.

Richard didn't like the first listing, so I showed him a few more. One day, he asked if he could see a place on the West Side again and I said it wouldn't be a problem. I was headed to a dinner afterwards, but I could squeeze him in. I always overdressed a bit, and when I would go out in the evening I would really go nuts.

"This doesn't look like something a real estate agent would wear," Richard said. "Do you have a date tonight?"

It caught me off guard, but I just kind of laughed it off and went on with my day. I didn't consider Richard to be a serious love interest then. He had a girlfriend.

Richard ended up renting a town house on 63rd between Park and Madison. He was happy. I was happy. We parted ways. Then, six months later, he called my office.

"Dorinda, I have Richard Medley on the phone."

I answered the phone, unsure of what he wanted. "Hi, Richard, how's it going?"

"Well! Very well, actually!"

I remember asking the same question twice. "So, how's it going? What's up?"

He told me he'd broken up with his girlfriend. And then he asked me out. "I was wondering if you'd like to go out with me tomorrow night to the opening of the Time Warner building?"

Yes, I wanted to date Richard, now that he was single. He seemed like a wonderful person. But I didn't like that he had given me only twenty-four hours' notice for a date. I was a single mother and he knew it. I talked about Hannah all the time. If we were going out on a date I would need time to get a babysitter, and I'm not the type of woman to scramble. Also, I was already going to the opening with my girlfriends, but that was beside the point.

"No," I said. "I have a daughter. If you want to ask a single mother out on a date, you should really ask her a week in advance so she can get a babysitter."

"How about three weeks from tomorrow?"

"Very funny. I have to go."

"Is that 'Dorinda speak' for yes?"

At some point he said good-bye and I hung up the phone, neither of us having agreed to a date. To be honest, I didn't take him too seriously because I just wasn't in the dating mind-set. My life was all about work and Hannah.

Anyway, the following evening, there I was at this Time Warner party talking away at the bar with my girlfriends when all of a sudden I felt a tap on my shoulder.

When I turned around and saw Richard, I thought, *Oh no.* It was such a big party that somehow I thought we might not run into each other.

"I see you got a babysitter for your daughter," he said.

"I told you I have a daughter, not that I didn't have a babysitter."

We laughed hysterically and ended up talking all night.

At some point, he asked, "Would you be available a week from today for a date?"

This time, I said yes.

Everything in life has a beginning,
a middle, and an ending. God controls the timeline.
(This one is courtesy of my mother, Diane Cinkala.)

Chapter Six

BECOMING MRS. MEDLEY

For our first date, Richard brought me to TAO.

I *hate* TAO. It's too big, too young, too loud, and it's really not my style. I was a mother, not a twenty-five-year-old who wanted to wear a short dress and party with the girls. I was more of a dinner party type. I didn't want to have to yell in order to hear myself speak.

What makes the Upper East Side so beautiful is how light it is. I don't know why, maybe it has something to do with the streets being wider or the buildings being shorter, but you can feel it the moment you arrive at the edge of Central Park. It's like one of those old Claritin commercials where a frosty film peels off the screen. TAO is the opposite of the Upper East Side. It looks like a dungeon, with a big dark door sporting those red-lit letters.

The centerpiece of the restaurant is the giant buddha inside, which is probably twenty feet high. Embedded within the seating chart of a restaurant is a hierarchy system that no one really talks about, but everyone can feel. At TAO, the closer you are to the Buddha, the higher up you are in the food chain.

The waiter brought us to our table, and it was right next to the Buddha. I looked over at Richard and he had a big grin on his face and his arm out. "Well, look at this!" I quickly realized that Richard, like me, didn't really frequent places like TAO, and I assumed he'd probably pulled some strings to get us this spot. He looked so pleased with himself, but totally out of place, too, which only made me like him more.

No matter where you were with Richard, he had a way of making you feel like the center of the universe. There are those people who, regardless of whether you are or you aren't special, make you feel like what you have to say matters, even in the most unexciting situations. Richard was one of those people. His gift was his ability to carve out little nooks in crowded spaces for you to be heard. Where you came from and what you had didn't matter as much as the fact that you had something to say, and Richard made it his business to hear it. You could really be yourself with him because there was no penalty for contradicting yourself. He was never shocked by anything, only ever curious and empathetic. He didn't hold grudges or dish out judgment.

A few dates in, I got honest with Richard: "I'm not interested in a lover, Richard Medley. I want a life partner. I want a best friend. I want someone I can count on no matter what. I'm a mother, first and foremost; do you get that?"

That was something I used to repeat constantly: "I'm a mother."

I never explained what it meant and didn't feel like I needed to. If he didn't get it, there was nothing more to talk about. I was never going to have my daughter wake up with some stranger in our kitchen. I would always choose her over everything and everyone else. Dating me meant accepting that you would always be second, and that was hard for some men.

"I do understand," Richard said. "I *really* do." He had kids himself, so I believed him.

Not long after TAO, Richard invited me to the Met Gala. *The Met Gala.* I nearly died. But in the same hour he invited me, he also shot himself in the foot. Within thirty minutes of me saying yes, several dresses arrived at my apartment. I called him up and pretended like I hadn't even opened them.

I didn't want to give Richard the impression that I was a woman who needed to be dressed for an event—because I wasn't that woman. I was familiar with how to appear at fabulous events. I'd been hanging out at Buckingham Palace! And so I said, "Richard, I am not six years old. Do you not trust me? Do you think I'll wear jeans to the Met Gala?"

Really, this was a test. If Richard was an asshole, he would have dumped me right then. But he wasn't an asshole. "I thought it would be a nice gesture," he said. "But I don't care what you wear. I just want to spend the evening with you."

I ended up wearing my own Alexander McQueen gown—which was made by Alexander McQueen himself. It was so on point. All night, Richard kept checking the time to make sure I wouldn't be late for Hannah's babysitter. This was more evidence that he truly understood my life and wanted to be a part of it.

The morning after the ball, I woke up to the most enormous bouquet of flowers. It was so big that it needed to be hauled up to my apartment on a luggage cart. Hannah, who was ten years old at the time, saw it and said, "Momma, I think this one really likes you."

"I think this one really likes me, too," I said.

Richard was giving and amenable. He asked me out a lot and didn't mind when I said no. He made things convenient for me. He had two children—Paige, fourteen, and Aidan, eight—from his previous marriage. Paige went to school at Spence, which was across the street from Hannah's school. If I wasn't available in the evening, Richard would say, "Why don't we meet before school to drop off the girls and just have a coffee?" Or, if I said no to a dinner, he'd invite me to breakfast. We spent many mornings at the Carlyle Hotel eating the most beautiful breakfasts together.

After about three months of us dating, Richard met Hannah. We went to a restaurant for french fries and chicken fingers. They hit it off like a house on fire. Hannah was like a chameleon. How much she revealed was based on how comfortable she felt with the person. She was her biggest self almost instantly. I had literally warned Richard about her being shy, and she was pretty much giving a TED Talk to Richard on lemurs that very first night.

Watching Hannah and Richard form a bond made my heart sing. They quickly became incredibly close, so much so that I sometimes felt like a third wheel. He and Hannah used to sit together and read for hours. Hannah was a questioner and Richard had all the patience that I didn't have to help her find the answers. From the moment they met, there was an overwhelming sense that Richard and Hannah had known each other for decades. It didn't take long for me to realize that Richard Medley was meant to be in my life. The way he loved my daughter made me love him even more. There was never a sense that it was Richard and me, with Hannah on the side. It was all of us, together.

Ralph also loved Richard. They'd met many times, and Ralph's wife was also now a part of the family, and a big part of Hannah's life. Richard and Ralph had Hannah in common; they had shared interests. They bonded over the ancient Greeks. "Ralph, I hear you're rethinking the philosophy of Aristotle," Richard would say, and I would wonder how I had gotten here. What were these people talking about? I might not have known, exactly, but I appreciated that it was bringing them closer. On some level, I think what bonded Richard and Ralph most was their love of Hannah. There was never a sense of jealousy or competition. It was as though they both recognized that they each had important roles to play in her life, and that made all the difference.

As time went on, Richard and I became inseparable. I started going to his house in the Hamptons even though I hate the Hamptons, and Richard started coming up to the Berkshires with me. He met my parents, who adored him. I showed him the house on the hill I'd always wanted to buy: Blue Stone Manor.

And then one day he bought it for me.

"I want you to have something that has nothing to do with me," he said.

Once it became clear that Richard and I would get married, Ralph and I officially divorced. On the day the divorce papers finally came through, Richard and I looked at each other and realized that there was no longer anything stopping us from tying the knot. And so we called a minister and got married in the living room.

But it wasn't until later that we were publicly married—in a huge celebration that spanned an entire weekend. It was fantastic. First, we got married at the Brick Church. Richard was actually a deacon there. It was a Presbyterian church, which was a lot more relaxed than the Catholic churches I was used to. When I went for the first time I thought, *Where's all the ceremony?* I love rituals. I love the dance of Catholicism. You stand; you sit; you kneel; you do it all over again. It's kind of like the Hokey Pokey. Presbyterians don't do this. They stay seated for communion and dress like they're at the country club. Over time, I came to appreciate Richard's church, and more, I loved who he was at church. He became his most Ohioan self, shaking hands and greeting people like he lived in a small town.

It was a beautiful, traditional wedding. I wore an elegant custom-made gown in champagne silk. We held the reception and dinner at The Grill in the iconic Seagram Building in New York City, and transformed it into a water-inspired wonderland. The 1920s architecture of the restaurant is stunning, as are the details of the main room. At the center is the fountain area, and all around the room the windows are covered by blinds made of superlight transparent beads that look like water when they move. I hired the supertalented Bronson van Wyck as my wedding planner, and together we took this water theme and ran with it. I should tell you that Richard loved the water, so much so that he kept his Hinckley yacht in New York from April to November. It had a sleeping cabin, so we'd sometimes take weekend trips together to the Hamptons, or we'd just cruise around the Statue of Liberty. I never felt more in love with Richard than I did when we were sharing a glass of wine on the back of the boat. It was as if when we were on the boat nothing else mattered.

In the spirit of our water-inspired theme, we turned the entire restaurant into an enormous aquarium by installing projectors to give the impression that fish were swimming around the room. Instead of flowers, we had fish in glass balls filled with water and suspended from the ceiling over the dining tables, and we covered the tables with huge Victorian-style vases—all of which were filled with fish. We built a stage behind a series of curtains that opened up at different times, and behind them we installed an opera singer, a Frank Sinatra impersonator, and an aerialist, who all gave performances throughout the dinner service. It was whimsical, lighthearted, and fun.

Richard stood up during the dinner and gave a beautiful and moving speech that ended with him saying, "You are my due north, always there to guide me. No matter how stormy it gets, I look to my due north."

There was never a day that I wasn't proud to be Mrs. Medley. Richard wore many hats and had lived what seemed like a hundred lives. He'd grown up outside Columbus, Ohio. His father was a train conductor and his mother a stay-at-home mom. He had worked his way up the old-fashioned way, slow and steady. After joining the Air Force, he went to Ohio State on the GI Bill. He went to Yale for graduate school, where he earned a PhD in philosophy, and after working as a Democratic speech writer and as a consultant for George Soros, Richard started his own company, Medley Global Advisors. Basically, what he did all day was geopolitical analysis. The goal was to analyze information, then write up a report, which he would then sell to hedge funds and banks, who used it to inform their trades in the stock market. At the time, I didn't realize how unique this was. There hasn't really been anyone else who has done what Richard did.

When he first took me to his office for Medley Global Advisors, I thought it was like a playhouse. There were arcade games and Ping-Pong tables, and offices were spread out across an open floor plan. There was a chef who would come cook lunch for the team and a massage therapist for the employees to use to reduce stress. If someone needed to bring their child to work, Medley Global Advisors would call a babysitter to come take care of the child at the office. This was way before Google or Facebook, and to me (and most others) it was a wild concept.

Richard understood the importance of community and collaboration and valued that above all else. He was never someone who breathed down his employees' backs or sent cold emails. As a boss, he believed that the key to success was creating an environment where people felt valued and comfortable. He turned the office into a place where you *wanted* to go. And meanwhile, he was in the business of making predictions that would fundamentally shape how some of the world's biggest financial powerhouses acted. He made it look easy. For all the pressure, you never saw a crack.

My life with Richard was incredibly dynamic. We traveled a lot and spent a good amount of time in Washington, DC, where Richard seemed to know people from all walks of life. The draw of this wasn't power or nice things, necessarily. It was seeing Richard interact with people with whom he felt a mutual trust and regard. Richard was a person who could command the attention of people who commanded the attention of others, and he did it without puffing his chest out or making a spectacle. Great people like Henry Kissinger would pull Richard aside at cocktail parties to pick his brain. The best thing about Richard, though, was that he had no airs. He treated Henry Kissinger in the same way he treated the valet guy. Richard truly valued every person equally. He used to say, "Everyone has a lesson to teach you."

As important as he was, Richard always made me feel like *I* was the important and indispensable element in our equation. Standing next to him, I was never arm candy or "the wife." We were partners in life and love. It was an honor to be his wife.

My attraction to Richard was one I'd never experienced before. It was physical, spiritual, and mental: the whole package. From the very start, we understood each other. It felt comfortable and familiar. It was as if I'd known him for a long time. It was an intense connection, a fire that burned hard and fast.

Richard had a relentless belief in the power of possibility and it had everything to do with his success. The entire world could be falling apart and Richard would be sitting in his chair with his laptop, writing a report contemplating the possibilities that the moment presented. He was like a trunk of a tree, the part that keeps the tree in place when it's whipped around by the worst of storms, and this was great for me, because I worry about everything.

At some point, a few years into my relationship with Richard, I was asked to be a Housewife. I knew some of the women on the show. We traveled in the same circles. Richard wanted me to do it, but I said no. I wanted to devote myself to being his wife and Hannah's mother. I didn't want to devote myself to being on television or, quite frankly, to anything other than my new life with Richard and our now-blended families. It simply didn't fit into my life at that point.

For the next few years, life moved fast. We lived mostly in New York and went to the Berkshires as often as possible. We decided to purchase a place in the Bahamas. I was busy running our lives and redoing both of our homes, and Richard was busy with work. We had all sorts of people over to the house for parties and dinners and other events that I would plan. This was when everything I'd learned in London really came in handy. I am great at planning a party, and Richard knew that. He would defer to me. He trusted me to take care of this realm of our lives.

Our dinner guests included prime ministers, political figures, special agents from the CIA, actors, singers, speakers. Hillary Clinton came to dinner, as did Desmond Tutu, Angelina Jolie and Brad Pitt, and Norah Jones. Richard was friends with the Kennedys. Richard knew all these people I was in awe of—people who made even *me* nervous—and he made it look so casual. No matter who you were or what you had, you always got the same Richard. When he spoke to you, he really spoke *with* you. And in those moments, however long or short, you became the center of his universe.

Honestly, it made me jealous sometimes. I was used to being the life of the party, and now that was my husband. And yet, when Richard was away on business or out of the house for too long, I really missed him. I wanted to be around him all the time. He was fun, and he was my partner and husband and I loved spending time with him.

In a lot of ways, he was all the things I wanted to be. He was freethinking and fun-loving, and he found the good in everything and everyone. He could see light in the darkest of rooms, and create an expanse in the smallest of places. Just by being his wife, my life became brighter, and my world became bigger.

But, I repeat, Richard was more fun than I was. Sometimes *too* fun. That meant I had to be stricter to compensate for his lack of discipline. With the kids, he was always the good guy, and I became the villain. I accepted the role because I thought it was best for my family, but I certainly had less fun than he did.

The kids loved Richard because he was like a kid himself. He'd be advising Ben Bernanke in the morning, and in the afternoon he'd be coordinating Ping-Pong competitions and playing paintball with his kids. He would dance and dress up in costumes. One day, he dressed up in a bear costume and knocked on the door while I was in the kitchen cooking. I opened the door and there he was, my important husband, dressed like an animal for no reason.

Richard somehow became a VIP everywhere he went, including Kmart. He used to take the kids there like it was Bergdorf Goodman. They called it The Great Kmart Adventure. The employees knew him. The manager would come out and say, "Hello, Mr. Medley, how many carts will you be needing today?"

Can you guess what my response was to this?

"Stop spending so much money at Kmart!"

So, Richard was fun and I was a police officer. Richard was Disney and I was the IRS. He was always on the hunt for the next adventure, and some of our adventures were lavish. He would book the craziest trips. He booked a boat for a week to take us around the Bahamas. He took my parents, Hannah, and me on a trip through Europe. We spent New Year's in the Maldives in pavilions on stilts hovering over the water. We flew in private planes. I needed only to look at something in the window of a store and he would buy it for me a day later.

I wanted to make sure Hannah maintained some sense of reality, but Richard made it hard. He didn't make any of these lavish choices for himself, though. The joy of his success was rooted in his ability to share it with others. I think that's the part of it that kept Hannah somewhat normal. There was always a sense of giving and gratitude that came with everything we did, and there was, too, Richard himself, who didn't put a lot of stock in nice things. He was a man who was thoroughly content eating macaroni from a box or peanut butter and jelly sandwiches with no crusts, his favorite. The constant acknowledgment of how special our experiences were brought awareness to the fact that it wasn't normal. And if I ever sensed any entitlement in Hannah, I vigilantly nipped it in the bud.

Hannah had a mixture of basic and extravagant clothes growing up. I never did the in-between. Either we were going to H&M or she was getting something special to treasure for as long as it fit. (In fact, she still wears some things from her teenage years to this day.) Normally, Hannah appreciated her things and treated them well. Once, however, while on holiday in Aspen, Hannah, while trying frantically to get dressed, shoved every article of clothing under her bed in a massive wrinkled pile. What she didn't realize was that she hadn't properly tucked it away. As I was walking by her room, I noticed a piece of clothing peering out from under the bed skirt. When I found all the beautiful clothes that I'd bought her tossed under the bed, I took most of them to the Goodwill. When she came home, I acted as though nothing had happened. Then, about five minutes after she went up to her room, she came bounding down the steps in a panic.

"What happened to my clothes, Mom? All my clothes are gone!"

"Well, did you put them away nicely?"

Her face went red.

"You obviously don't value what you have, and seem to think

that it is disposable and not worth taking care of, so I gave them away to someone who would appreciate them."

Hannah lost her mind and begged to earn the clothes back. There was no earning them back, though. I told her she had everything she needed: her school uniform, several outfits for special occasions, a couple pairs of jeans, T-shirts, sweatshirts, a few nice sweaters, a few nice pairs of shoes, boots, and a pair of sneakers. For months after that, Hannah wore white T-shirts and jeans on repeat, and she put them away very neatly in her closet when she wasn't wearing them.

While I tried to keep Hannah down-to-earth, I went wild renovating Blue Stone Manor—possibly a little wilder than I should have. I hired my dear friend the interior decorator Marshall Watson to help me bring the house back to its glory. Marshall knew me and understood my vision for the house, and over the next three years we painstakingly reviewed every inch and every detail together. Phil Timpane was the lead contractor on the project, and because he is an artist himself he was a huge asset in bringing our visions to life. What could be restored was restored and what could be replicated by an artisan was replicated. We went through hundreds of drawings, pictures, paint colors, and fabrics. Marshall Watson and I spent many nights walking through the grounds with a bottle of wine, discussing ideas.

Blue Stone Manor sits on eighteen acres. When we bought the house, there was zero landscaping. It was just an open plot of land. Lucky for me, Marshall is not only a fantastic interior decorator. He's also an expert landscaper.

As you approach the hedge-lined entrance and enter the gates of Blue Stone Manor (which I designed) the first thing you see is a huge cornfield. This sort of protects the house and adds to the country manor feel. The landscape includes beautiful hedges that surround the house, amazing hyacinths and lilac bushes, a hedged pathway that leads to the cornfields, and a small maze—which we felt would add not only a sense of whimsy but also a sense of being, perhaps, in Europe rather than in Great Barrington.

I left the basic structure of the house as it was, and on top of that, I added my own creative strokes. Living abroad for ten years had made my personal tastes more interesting and daring. I took inspiration from my visits to country houses in England and from my time traveling through Europe. While living abroad, I was exposed to new sensibilities, which included taking risks with color and with decorating. And so, Blue Stone Manor is designed with all this in mind. It's a house filled with curiosities. Some people like it. Some people don't. But either way, it's always a fun conversation piece.

I told Marshall and Phil that I wanted the vibe to be Frankenstein-meets–Marilyn Monroe. I covered the closets in silver foil wallpaper; I painted a hallway black; I even had the famous Douglas Little design this amazing chandelier made of animal skulls and diamonds and pearls to hang in the black hallway. My house is full of surprises, and it's also completely utilitarian. The kitchen is designed after the old working kitchens of England. It's not glamorous. It's made for actual cooking. Every room at Blue Stone Manor gets used, and every room is distinct and original.

Blue Stone Manor is not a house that is precious. It's a house that's designed to be lived in, and there are separate spaces for reading, playing games, cooking, eating, and lounging. Often, when guests come for the weekend, they have lots of outside plans, but what happens is they pull up the driveway on Friday and don't leave the house until Sunday afternoon.

Renovations took three years, and once they were done we finally moved back into Blue Stone Manor. I cooked big dinners. Richard wrote in his office. We had cocktails out on the patio overlooking the great lawn. We spent the first couple of years in that house just allowing ourselves to be awestruck by the environment we had created. Because I had designed it, the house naturally reflected me. But Richard's presence was embedded into Blue Stone Manor, too. He was like the heartbeat of the house. Every time I think of parting with Blue Stone Manor—keeping it up is a job in and of itself and who needs all this space?—I stop myself because it is the place where I feel Richard's presence most viscerally. Sometimes when I sit outside and watch the sunset, I get a bizarre impulse to open my palm up on the arm of my chair, as if the gesture would be met by the person who was meant to hold my hand.

Though our days together were full, the years passed quickly. Sooner than I could have thought to expect it, Richard changed. His presence lost its gentle majesty, like a fading flame holding on to the last weave of a wick. He dulled, no longer answering my questions with the same keen sense of self or telling stories with his clever sharpness. His skin took on a yellow tinge. More frightening than anything else, though, was that he refused to go to the doctor, no matter how much I begged. It was as though he knew it was bad and wanted to hold on to the last pieces of our life together before they could be cast in the shadow of an ending. Our sun had begun to set, and my life became about watching the sky fade to black.

When Richard started losing a lot of weight, I got so nervous that I developed a shake in my hand. I had a total meltdown, and Richard promised he would go to the hospital if I took him from New York to the Berkshires one last time. He was so weak that I had to call Richard's barber, Steve Violet, who, at six feet seven and weighing 250 pounds, looks more like a bodyguard for the Hells Angels than a barber, to come over and carry Richard out of bed and onto the patio overlooking the property. We sat there quietly holding hands, at random moments looking at each other and shedding a tear or two. We didn't say it, and up until the last possible moment I pretended like it was going to be okay, but we knew. This was the last seed of life Richard had to plant at my feet before our beautiful garden lost its green.

We went to the hospital and they admitted him immediately. And then it became a domino effect of health issues. One thing went wrong; then another thing went wrong. If it wasn't his kidneys, it was his blood pressure. If it wasn't his blood pressure, it was his liver. All his vital organs were shutting down so fast that soon the details about what was wrong stopped mattering. The disintegration of a human is humiliating. No matter what accomplishments you have had, at the end of the day you are just a body. No one cares what your last name is or what parties you went to or who you know. It is isolating, heartbreaking, and horrifyingly impersonal.

The sicker he got, the more Richard tried to distance himself from me, and even though I knew it wasn't personal, it was still painful at times. I started to realize that he was no longer Richard and, more important, that with each day I was less and less his wife. I still needed to keep it together, though. Every time I felt like falling apart, I told myself, *Be strong; you can do this. Hannah needs you.* I kept up appearances for the kids, because I didn't want them to know how far Richard had declined.

Our existence became a chaotic concerto of life and death. Out of nowhere blood would start oozing out of Richard's ears and eyes and mouth and they would have to take him to surgery. They would put a respirator down his throat, which he hated more than anything. Every time we thought it might be over, he would pull through again. Then he would bleed again. And pull through again. This went on for months. Hannah, who was eighteen, would go through periods where she would spend every waking moment with him in the ICU, literally writing her college applications by his side or asking her SAT tutor to do their sessions in the hospital cafeteria. Then she would disappear for a week and talk to me on the phone about regular life things as if nothing tragic were happening. I had no manual for how to handle Richard's death. All I could do was my best. We were all just trying to survive.

One night when I was taking a bath, a feeling of immense dread came over me. I got in bed, turned all the lights on, and pretended to watch television. When Hannah came to my bedroom, as she did every night, and asked me what was wrong, I told her that I was feeling strange. "I'm not sure why," I said, "but I think we need to go to the hospital."

We got dressed, hailed a cab, and went to the hospital. When we arrived, Richard was awake and alert—much more than usual. For months it had been like he was in a conscious coma. Even hearing him talk about some delusion was enough to make us hopeful. But that night, he wasn't delusional. He was himself. We laughed and talked about what we were going to do when we got out of the hospital. After a couple hours, Hannah and I left. I can remember her saying to me, "You just knew it, Mom. Aren't you glad we went?"

The next morning, Richard had his last bleed. I called the family in. Hannah was there, and Paige, Aidan, Bob (Richard's brother), my friend Anne, and Ralph. The doctors took me into a small room with yellow walls and a picture of a waterfall. They told me, "This is as bad as it gets."

I was then told that I had two options. Either I could choose to operate on Richard again to try to stop the internal bleeding, with no real hope of long-term success, or I could choose to put him into a morphine-induced coma.

What?

Because I had power of attorney, I was left to make these decisions. There were no good choices left anymore, because either way it was probably going to be the end. The doctors informed me that any measure would prolong his life by no more than a couple of days and likely be traumatic. I didn't want that for Richard. I didn't want him to die on a surgery table or in another massive bleed, so as his conservator I made the incredibly difficult decision to reject further invasive surgery.

For the next couple of hours, Richard's breathing faded to a raspy gurgle. This is a sound that's commonly known as the "death rattle." It's what happens when a person can no longer swallow and the saliva pools at the back of their throat. As we sat there with Richard, this sound got quieter and quieter, and the world became more and more still.

And then, out of nowhere, I heard this voice whoosh up my body like a wind: *I'm out of here.*

I turned to everyone and said, "He's gone."

The fight was over. What had been the longest three months of my life ended like the flash of a camera. It was shockingly uneventful. One second Richard was there, and the next second he wasn't. I walked out of the room in a bizarre state. Was it grief? Or was it something else? It was as if someone had handed me a massive boulder to hold and then walked away and there I was asking, *What do I do with this? Where do I even put it?*

You don't feel what you think you're going to feel in those first hours. As horrible as this may sound and as guilty as it may make me feel, on some level I think I was relieved. I'd dropped to 106 pounds; my hair was falling out; I hadn't slept for months. Hannah had spent the past few months pretending on and off like everything was fine, which somehow felt heavier than the weight I had lost. There was no hope left. But there was also nothing left to fear. All that was left was, well, nothing.

That night, Hannah and I ordered a pizza and fell into a deep sleep in my bed. At some point, I was jostled out of my sleep by the sound of her crying. Her back was turned to me, so I inched over and wrapped my arm around her waist, allowing the sudden pulse of her breath to expand and contract against my chest. We had loved and lived so much, and now we had lost so much. Somewhere in between guilt and grief, it all hit me at once, and I started to cry, too.

In life, you have to accept that all things
happen for a reason, both good and sometimes bad.

Chapter Seven

NOW WHAT?—AGAIN

Richard hadn't wanted anyone to know he was sick, so I had to keep it a secret, which was horrible. Every once in a while I would go to some event to keep up appearances. Coming up with reasons for why Richard wasn't there with me was such a painful performance that it sometimes made me sick. The secret of his dying was like a small creature that I had swallowed live.

And then, the morning after his death, I opened up the *Wall Street Journal* and the *Times* and many other publications both in print and online, and there it was: "Richard Medley, dead at age 60."

I was now a forty-six-year-old widow.

Everyone called, wanting to know what had happened. The condolences poured in. "Oh my God, Dorinda, I'm so sorry. What can I do?"

I knew that everyone was coming from a good place and that they were processing the shock of his death, too. But to be honest I wanted to punch them in the face. What do you mean: "What happened?" He *died*. He's dead.

I was angry. Richard's illness had been like a bull let loose in the china shop of our life. His inability to reconcile himself with the imminence of his death made it impossible for me to prepare for it. There was no opportunity to prolong his life because the hope of something more was less palatable than the fantasy of what was. I knew how frightened he was of death and my impulse was to console him rather than spark up a discussion about wills and funerals. So there I was at the end, reckoning with all the details on my own.

For all the decisions you are forced to make, none of them give you any sense of control. In fact, the chaos is in the questions: *Do I donate his eyes? Do I donate his kidneys? What casket should I get? Do I let people look at his body? Who's going to carry the casket down the aisle? Where will the reception be afterwards? What's everyone going to eat? What am I going to do without him? What now?*

I decided against a wake because I didn't want people to see how much he'd deteriorated. The decision was a vestige of my protective impulse and my desire to keep him alive by honoring what I assumed would have been his wish. I decided to bury the evidence of who he had become because it was a freckle on the face of who he was.

We had the funeral at the same place we'd been married: the Brick Church. As I was walking down the aisle behind the pallbearers, all I could think was, *The last time I did this I was in a wedding dress.* That's really the worst part of the funeral, when you have to walk behind your husband's casket and watch everyone watching you. You want people to be there, but at the same time you don't, because the only thing worse than bearing the burden of your own grief is bearing the burden of everyone else's. I smiled and tried to look as many people in the eye as I could, but the truth is that I wasn't *really* there. I was with Richard; I was at our wedding.

Hannah gave the most beautiful speech at the funeral service, and I want to share a part of it with you:

Losing Richard broke me. An awful irreparable crack split me in two. At eighteen I realized that I had experienced the best and the worst moment of my life. I was given a world when I stood next to my mom and Richard at the altar of the Brick Church, and that same world was ripped away from me when we stood at the same altar feet away from his coffin. People say time heals all wounds, but it doesn't. I'll always feel like something is missing. Everything good I achieve is colored by his absence. That sounds very sad and feels very sad to say, but isn't it also kind of beautiful? That you can love someone so much they change you forever? That I can stand here today and say that I am who I am because of who he was. Death is painful, death is difficult, but death gives you boundaries to life. It gives love a shape and a form. It gives meaning to our experiences. I always say if a song didn't have an ending, it would just be noise. And ending gives a moment a meaning. So today, in the words of Dr. Seuss, "Don't cry because it's over. Smile because it happened."

We buried Richard at St. Peter's Cemetery, in the plot that my parents had bought for themselves. I didn't tell many people about the burial. In the end, it was just my mom and dad; my sister; the kids; our housekeeper, Len; our dogs, Lucy and Evie; a priest; and a couple of local people. Quite frankly, Richard would have approved. We had the big funeral in New York with tons of people, and then the quiet burial in Great Barrington. He would have thought it was perfect.

There was evidence of Richard scattered all over the house. His colorful cashmere socks, his many pairs of Stubbs & Wootton loafers—they all had fun sayings on them—his coffee mugs, and, most devastatingly, his signature collection of wacky reading glasses, all of them colorful, some of them covered in bling. Richard never wanted to be more than an arm's length away from his reading glasses, so they were everywhere. (To this day, I will open a drawer and find a pair.) Going back to the house was like seeing a portrait of a now-past life. I canceled the credit cards and then I put them in a box, along with his passports and his driver's license and the other things I couldn't bear to throw away yet. I took all his clothes out of the closet right away and put them up in the attic. I worried that if I left his things out, it would make me too sad.

It was bizarre to become a widow, and the term didn't feel right to me. When I thought of widows, I imagined very old ladies dressed in black. I was only forty-six years old. After all the ceremony and after all the shock of his death wore off, I realized that a big part of my identity had been completely wrapped up in my role as Richard's wife. Who was I without that? I felt lost. So I did the only thing I knew to do. I just kept moving forward. I gave this movement a name, too: Operation Normalize.

Just two weeks after the funeral, I had my entire family up to the Berkshires for Thanksgiving. It would have been a shame to skip it. In fact, Richard would have been highly disappointed. He loved a good gathering, and he knew how happy it made me to be surrounded by friends and family.

During this time, I drank, and too heavily, to self-medicate. I was in so much pain. But still, I was taking care of business. I had to. Operation Normalize also meant that I would execute the wishes in Richard's will and shut down his business as quickly as possible. I went into overdrive, needing to put this chapter of my life behind me. I felt judged for not crying all the time, which is what we expect widows to do. People want you to be sad and mournful. They take pity on you. My basic reaction to pity at the time was, "Aw, thank you, I'm fine!" Approaching the topic of death is awkward, and maybe in a way I wanted to make people feel better about how awkward it was.

Richard had made me the executor of the estate. I understood why he'd done that, but it was also daunting and scary and something I was not fully prepared for. It was a big responsibility, and I had to be extremely dedicated to handling it carefully, because it also included his children.

Executing Richard's wishes meant that for months I was surrounded by lawyers and estate people. They were mostly men, and it was business as usual for them. There was little room for gentleness around Richard's death and my grief. A lot of these men treated me like I was helpless, which made things more difficult. I wasn't helpless. I was willing to do whatever I needed to do to get things done.

Even if I wasn't prepared emotionally, I was overly prepared from an accounting angle. I had every check we'd ever written, in shoe boxes, filed by month. Since it was business as usual for the lawyers and the estate people, I treated it like a business, too. I interacted with no emotions, because that's what I needed to do to get through it. It wasn't that I didn't *have* emotions. I did. I was straightforward and professional and slightly cold during every meeting I went to concerning Richard's estate—and then sometimes I'd get into my Uber and just burst into tears, not so much out of fear but more because of extreme grief and exhaustion. During this time, I was taking care of the tasks I could take care of, but inside, I felt consumed by grief. My world had been turned upside down. I was grasping for anything that felt familiar.

When Richard was admitted to the hospital, I moved out of the town house and back into my apartment on the Upper East Side. I think on some level, I knew he would never be coming back. In one way, it was reassuring. In another way, I felt like I was moving backwards. I was alone again, and while the old walls of that apartment were a comfort to me, my life had changed so drastically that everything felt unrecognizable, including myself. Who was I now? And what was I going to do next?

In order to fully understand where I was emotionally during this time, I need to tell you a little more about what my relationship with Richard was like. We were the type of couple that did everything together. And by "everything," I really do mean everything. I chose his outfits in the morning; I booked his appointments; I was involved in his business. During every moment of every day, I knew what Richard was doing and he knew what I was doing. Was this healthy? I honestly don't know, but it's the way it was. Our lives were completely enmeshed.

What this meant was that over the course of our relationship I had had less time for friends. It was totally unlike my marriage to Ralph. With Ralph, I'd had tons of time to cultivate and expand my friendships. And at all other points in my life, too, friendship had played a huge role. But while I was with Richard, I kind of just stopped calling my girlfriends as much. I let my supportive circle of women drift to the wayside. This was, in retrospect, a mistake, and there's a big lesson here: keep your friends close and don't put all your eggs in one basket, because you don't know what is going to happen. After Richard's death, I felt so incredibly lonely. I felt like I was on an island by myself. I still had Hannah, but Hannah was grown now, on the verge of going off to college, and grieving in her own way.

Slowly, I started to live again. I even started to laugh. I began to forget the images of sick Richard and started to miss who he'd been when he was healthy and happy. I looked through old photo albums with friends and family and reminisced about better times, and that was healing.

"Remember when Richard almost killed everyone chasing a rainbow?"

"Remember when he dressed up like a bear?"

"Remember Kmart?"

It felt good to be laughing again.

About four months after he died, a well-known psychic named Anne called me. I'd run into Anne at parties in Washington for years. She was a well-known character in DC and a longtime acquaintance of Richard's. She'd advised people like Nancy Reagan and Jackie Onassis. I was scared to pick up the phone at first. What if Anne had something negative to tell me? I ignored her calls, but she kept calling. She wouldn't stop. One night while I was drinking and crying about Richard, feeling incredibly lonely, I finally picked up.

"I'm so glad I've gotten ahold of you!" Anne said. "Richard has been contacting me nonstop because he needs to give you a message."

"Is he okay?"

Let me pause here and tell you that for the first few weeks after Richard died he was around. I know how that sounds, but it's true. I could feel his presence, and I thought that he was there because he was struggling to move on to the next step. I thought he didn't want to leave me, but he had to. So, about two months into this, I spoke to him: "You need to move on, Richard. Go!" Soon after that, I didn't feel his presence anymore. He was gone.

Now, here's what Anne said to me on the phone:

"First of all, Richard wants you to know he loves you. He also wants you to know that he's sorry for scaring you, but he didn't want to go. He couldn't figure out why all those people were at the

Brick Church. He wanted to be part of it. He wasn't happy about leaving. But now he's transcended. And he's doing great. He wants me to tell you that you'll always be his north. Last, if you ever need to talk to Richard, he'll be listening."

I could not believe this conversation! How had she known that Richard was around and then he wasn't? The due north thing—it was possible she'd heard that from other people or that it had been printed somewhere, but still. I was floored. And it gave me peace to have someone remind me that I could still talk to Richard. I never had to be completely without him.

When I told this story to my mother, she reminded me of how, when Richard and I used to take two helicopters to Hyannisport—he with his children, me with mine—we'd wave at each other in the sky. "You couldn't talk to him, but you knew he was there. It's like that now. Just think of him as being in the other helicopter."

So that's what I do. I talk to him out on the porch in the Berkshires. It gives me hope.

Besides the condolences and the judgment that I wasn't a sad enough widow, there was often the empty question, "How are you?" Nobody really wanted to know how I was. Death is heavy. It brings people down. They're afraid of it. They asked me that question, "How are you?," to be polite and I understood that, but it was also annoying. *How do you think I am?* People didn't want me to be lonely, but they were afraid of my loneliness, too, as if it might be contagious.

After a while, the unsolicited advice started pouring in. Some people thought I absolutely shouldn't date for a long time and other people said, "You should start dating soon." I had no plans to start dating soon. In the months after Richard's death, I was focused on Hannah, my home, my family, and close friends. I wanted to find some sort of rhythm again in this new life. Being Richard's wife had been so all-consuming and I had kind of forgotten how to be on my own.

One day, while an old friend and I were out to lunch at the Core Club, a man named John Mahdessian walked up to the table and said, "How's my pal Richard doing?"

Richard and I used to have drinks at the Core Club about once a week, and John was one of the people we often ran into there. He was the owner of Madame Paulette, a well-known high-end dry cleaner in New York, and he managed to save me from a terrible situation involving an expensive borrowed Cavalli dress a few years back. I'd borrowed the intricate $18,000 dress from Roberto Cavalli himself for a dinner at Buckingham Palace, and my girlfriend had spilled red wine on it. (The dinner, by the way, was for Prince Charles and hosted by my friend Fizzy, who invited me.) I was paralyzed. How was I going to fix this dress?

Madame Paulette, amazingly, restored the Cavalli gown back to its original condition. After that, John would often greet me and Richard at the Core Club and ask how the dress was doing and we'd chat in the courtyard over drinks. Richard liked John, and John liked Richard. It was all very casual and friendly. We didn't know each other *that* well, and that's why, in mid-March, when I ran into John, he didn't know that Richard had passed away.

"You didn't hear?" I said. "About Richard."

John was shocked. "Richard *died*?"

"He died in November."

John told me he was so sorry, and then he offered to take me out sometime. "Let's go for dinner," he said.

I agreed. We went out for one dinner, and then another, and then another, and soon we were dating. At the time, I thought it wouldn't last long. I had no idea it would turn into a six-year relationship.

John was the opposite of Richard in every way imaginable. If Richard was vanilla ice cream, then John was peanut butter ice cream. He was fun, free, and unserious, a larger-than-life playboy who reminded me of my Italian grandfather. He'd never been married; he had no kids. He was untethered, super fun, and rough around the edges. He was Mister Feel Good. He used to say to people, "I am the Sultan of Stain, the Maverick of Fabric." I thought that was so stupid but also somehow endearing. He was just boisterous. He talked fast and liked to dance. He also liked to be surrounded by people, and, until we became exclusive, a lot of those people were women.

John introduced me to an entirely new world, and he lived in a new world, too: Queens. That little bridge from Manhattan to Queens makes a big difference. The people are different. The sophistication and rigidity are gone. John was friends with a very colorful group. Early in our relationship, he invited me to a wedding at Oheka Castle on Long Island, a place I had not known existed. The bride and groom emerged from neon-colored smoke clouds, and I thought, *Boy, these people know how to have fun!*

Quite frankly, I hadn't had good old-fashioned fun in a long time. John's type of fun reminded me of the fun of my youth—the weddings at the VFW and the huge holiday dinners with tons of relatives and food. John was familiar to me. He danced in the crazy way my family danced. And he brought levity to my life at a time when I really needed it.

The biggest problem with John was that the people around me disapproved of him and constantly compared him to my late husband, Richard. John had never been married, and it seemed to me that he had no idea what it meant to be a parent. He was my age but, it seemed to me, living like he was in his thirties. With John, I either regressed or was having a ball being young again, and I didn't really care which it was. I wanted to stay up and laugh and dance and drink.

It was nice, too, spending time with groups of people who had no idea who I was. They didn't care about who I knew or what my past life was like. I was living in the present and, in a way, it was an escape from the pain and grief I was feeling. The crossover between my world and John's was fun for so many reasons, but sometimes it was also awkward.

When I brought him to the Berkshires for the first time, he was dumbfounded. He had no idea that my life was so lavish. I caught him taking pictures of the house and sending them to his friends in Queens, which I thought was weird, and I told him so. "Don't be weird, John."

I never let John sleep at my place when we were in the city. I barely ever slept at his place. The first time I did, I woke up at 4:00 a.m. and thought, *I'm in Queens. This doesn't feel right.* I slithered out of the bed and was crawling to the door when John said, "Where are you going?"

"I need to be home. This is wrong. I have to wake up in my bed, my apartment, on the Upper East Side. This is fine at night, but during the day? No."

After dating me for a little while, John stopped seeing other women. We fell in love. Our relationship continued to be defined by fun, laughter, and friendship. I believe my time with John helped to heal me, and it helped John to grow up and know what real love and commitment is.

Until this point, I'd appeared in the background of various parties and events that had been filmed for *The Housewives*, because I ran in the same circles as many of the women on the show. We all lived in the small fishbowl of the Upper East Side. We got our hair done at the same place; we went to the same bars; we ran into each other on the street.

A few years earlier, I'd declined the offer, even though Richard had wanted me to say yes. Now when I was asked, I honestly thought it was a sign from Richard: *Take this, Dorinda.*

Even though I'd started to live again and even though I was dating John, I was still grieving and still trying to find out who I was without Richard. I felt like I was floating, like my life had no rails, and then suddenly the opportunity to be a Housewife arrived, and it seemed to make sense. It was something to hold on to.

As I took stock of the other elements in my life, it seemed to make even more sense. I felt like I had two options. I could either live off what Richard had left me and become one of those Upper East Side women who spend their lives going to Pilates and lunch, or I could take what I had and do something with it. I could make my own income. This was a big draw for me. As you know, I like working and I like making my own money. I had no one to depend on now, and *The Housewives* was a path toward independence. Plus, Hannah would be in college soon, so that would leave me with an empty nest.

Really, this was the first time since my early twenties that I could do whatever the hell I wanted, and I was ready to take the leap. Who was I outside the roles of mother and wife? Who was I as just plain Dorinda? I wanted to find out.

Bravo asked me if I was interested in becoming a castmate, and you know the rest of this story. After a series of interviews and screen tests, they hired me. How could they not? It was an obvious fit. I ticked all the boxes. I was friends with the other Housewives, and I lived the type of New York life that was portrayed on the show. I also fit the bill physically. I dressed in fashionable clothes; I was well-groomed. I told myself I would try it for a year and if I didn't like it I'd quit.

The first time I ever filmed was at my friend's house. I didn't understand how the mike was supposed to be attached at first. It felt strange to have it pressed against my body, and sort of unnatural, and when the camera started rolling it really hit me: I had decided to be filmed for television. I felt suddenly nervous. What was I supposed to say? What was I supposed to be doing with my hands?

It's not easy to show up and be filmed, knowing that the whole world is going to have opinions on what you do and who you are. It takes a certain amount of courage. Also, I was in such a vulnerable position when I started the show. I was still grieving and still unsure about who I was and who I wanted to become.

The Housewives is not scripted, as I've mentioned, and there's no training that happens beforehand. You just show up and they attach a mike to you and say, "Go." And then you're there, in your friend's kitchen, with a camera moving around you.

Once we got started, I was very happy to find out that the presence of the camera didn't bother me one bit. I stopped feeling nervous almost immediately, and at some point I forgot we were even being filmed. I loved the camera and the camera loved me. My very first time filming was with Ramona in the Hamptons. We just started talking, as we had done for years. We talked about the other women on the show; we said some things about upcoming plans. I was authentically myself in that first scene, just as I would always be. I said and did whatever I wanted. I didn't have to be Dorinda Medley anymore, or Dorinda Lynch, or even Dorinda Cinkala. I wasn't a good person or a bad person. I was just Dorinda, warts and all, and wow, what a sense of relief I felt.

Despite my tough shell, I'm very sensitive, and normally I feel guilty and fearful, as we all do sometimes. But weirdly, with *The Housewives* I felt none of that. It was as if the show existed inside a bubble of freedom for me. I loved it, and I promptly got completely swept up in the process of making it, because it was impossible not to.

The first year, I didn't understand that every single choice matters. Your shoes matter; your shirts matter; your earrings matter. I was naïve. I came as I was. I didn't consider that fans would be clocking every wardrobe choice or that my wardrobe choices would be written about in magazines or by bloggers who would want to know where the clothes came from so they could tell other people to buy them. Some would even add a link on Instagram to make it easier for fans to purchase the clothes I'd worn. This is a common experience for reality stars during their first year. They think they're playing checkers, but really, it's a game of chess. They think it's linear, but in fact, it's cumulative.

But I didn't know that yet. I was just showing up and taking the job as seriously as I've taken all my other jobs. I arrived on time and in my regular clothes. I didn't have hair and makeup people like some of the other women.

Even though I was exhausted, I enjoyed the hectic schedule. It was new and exciting. I was thrilled to be doing something that was all mine. I was just having fun. Then, in December, filming was over, and that was a new shock—the shock of crickets chirping.

The whole production team moved to another show. I was no longer seeing all the faces I'd become accustomed to seeing every day for four months. I suddenly had no packed schedule and no car picking me up every day. The first time I got into a cab after that first season of filming, I'd become so used to being chaperoned that I literally forgot I had to tell the driver where I wanted to go. I'd gotten so used to eating out at restaurants, and now it was time to go to D'Agostino to buy my own food. It was a startling change. One day I was being miked and people were bringing me coffee, and the next day I was just some blond lady going to the grocery store for celery like everybody else.

From January through March, I was walking around the Upper East Side, same as usual. Nobody knew who I was. Nobody knew I'd just filmed the show. Some days, I'd forget the show even happened. It didn't feel real yet. Other days, I'd remember a moment during filming and think, *Oh no, I hope they don't use that.* Or I'd remember a moment but couldn't remember if I was miked or not. You'd think this wouldn't happen—forgetting whether or not a microphone is attached to you—but it does, and much more frequently than you might like.

So, there I was in 2015, out and about in the neighborhood after filming had ended. By April, I wasn't thinking much about it at all. And then the show premiered.

Watching that very first episode was nerve-racking! This is when I started to understand how time and story work in reality television. Fifteen hours of filming can be cut to twenty minutes—and intercut with other scenes featuring other characters to give the impression that it might have all happened simultaneously. You might make a sly comment during the filming of the show and think nothing of it. Then later, you might watch the episode and find that the other women on the show are referencing your sly comment continuously. So, a ripple effect can happen, and you can't predict it. You get to watch the episode only a few days before the audience and all you can do is sit back and watch it unfold.

I realized some other things, too. Being on television is like ther-apy, or at least it's a great way to see yourself clearly. In fact, you don't know anything about yourself until you've seen yourself on-screen. And let me tell you, it is nothing if not incredibly enlightening.

Before I was on the show, I considered myself to be a stylish woman who was somewhat attractive. Well, I was both shocked and humbled when I saw myself on television for the first time. I didn't like the way I looked; I didn't like the way I dressed; I had no idea how crooked my nose was. I was much heavier than I thought. I couldn't believe the way I walked. I didn't know I used my hands so much when I talked.

And this, in a nutshell, is why a first-year Housewife looks noth-ing like that same Housewife in her second year. After seeing your-self on television, you get it together, which is to say that you go, *Oh, this is why everyone else has a stylist and a makeup artist.* With greater awareness comes greater curation. I was definitely hiring people to help me look better the next year.

Other things I didn't notice about myself: I referenced my mother all the time. So many sentences began, "My mother says . . ." Also, I talked *a lot*! But I was funny, even funnier than I'd thought, so at least I had that going for me.

Even though there were a bunch of things I wanted to fix and change, I was proud of how I'd shown up as myself. It wasn't that I hadn't been an honest person before *The Housewives*. It was that I hadn't allowed myself to shine. I no longer had to pretend. I didn't have anything other than myself. I'd consciously or unconsciously tried to always do the right thing for other people in my life and now I could do what was best for me. I'd been playing the roles of mom and wife and daughter and society woman for about fifty years. Little did I know how all these roles would prepare me for my role as a cast member of *The Real Housewives of New York City*.

The Dorinda on the show is me, but it's an exaggerated version of me. By watching myself on television, I came to understand myself in a new way. And this went a lot deeper than the external stuff. Experiencing this exaggerated version of myself allowed me to feel more deeply into the contours of my identity. It gave me a better sense of who I was, both on- and off-screen.

After watching the first episode, I got the call from Bravo. It was time to start doing promos.

What was a promo, exactly?

That's how naïve I was. I barely understood what a promo entailed. My first appearance ever, if I remember correctly, was on a daytime talk show. Teresa Giudice from *The Real Housewives of New Jersey* was also a guest. I remember feeling, well, very much like a beginner. Answering questions about my life necessitated an entirely different set of skills from the ones I'd used to be filmed for the show. I wasn't just living my regular life. I was trying to sell the show to viewers, so I wanted to be entertaining. In order to do this well, you sort of have to adopt a persona, but I didn't get that yet. I was just happy to be there and amazed that anyone was asking me questions about my life at all. I felt a little bit famous and I liked it.

I obviously saw how fame had affected my castmates who'd been on the show for a while. They were known entities around the city. But somehow, I still couldn't quite grasp what it really meant to become famous or how thoroughly it would change my life.

Don't try to make an apple into an orange.

Chapter Eight

HOUSEWIVES

*E*very morning, I would take my dog Lucy out for a walk in pajama pants and a sweatshirt. My routine was to hit the fruit stand for a banana and then Starbucks for a coffee. The morning after the show premiered, I walked out of my apartment complex and two women in Lululemon spandex were standing on the street.

"Oh my God, it's Dorinda Medley!" one of them said.

"Can we take a picture with you?" the other one asked.

That was the moment I realized I couldn't walk around in pajamas anymore. I wasn't just Dorinda anymore. I was Dorinda the Real Housewife of New York City.

I knew that people in their apartments were watching the show, but I had no idea how many people until they stopped me, yelled out to me, or just smiled at me in a way that said, *I know you.* I was no longer anonymous. The Lululemon-clad women were who I imagined as the audience, but it turned out many people from all walks of life had seen the show: cabdrivers, pharmacists, salespeople, my dentist. It was such a stark change for me. One day I was just like anybody else walking down the street, and the next day people were screaming out, "Dorinda!"

Fame is, in a nutshell, very strange. It's the most enticing mistress you'll ever bring into your life. It's like a fantastic martini. You know you should only have one or two. But it's so delicious that you want to keep drinking it. If you do that, though, you get drunk. So, you have to keep it to two martinis. Otherwise, you start to believe in your own hype, and that leads to disaster.

Along with screaming my name, people would also scream the name of the show: *"Housewives!"* For fans, we're an integral part of the city. I felt proud to represent New York as a Housewife because it's such an aspirational place. I think it's also, for many people, a mysterious place, so to give them an inside look at my life in the city felt rewarding. I might be biased, but in my opinion, the New York City Housewives are special because of the city we live in. New York truly is our playground. It's a pedestrian city, so running into friends on the street happens all the time, especially on the Upper East Side. As Iman once famously said, "New York is not a city. It's a world." I love being a part of that in life and I loved being a part of that on-screen.

The New York Housewives are great reality stars because we're all unique. While we have many similarities—lifestyle, age, location— we're all quirky in our own ways. Think about each Housewife as an ingredient in a cake. Some ingredients are stronger than others and some are less so, but you need them all. If one of the ingredients is missing, then the cake is a failure.

I became known as the voice of reason; the truth teller; the giver of wisdom; the quick-witted, call it like I see it, transparent one. I let it all hang out and told it like I saw it. And this is how I am in real life, too. When fans meet me, they always say, "You're just like you are on the show!" Or they ask, "When can I come to Blue Stone Manor?"

When you're on reality television, the audience has seen you brushing your teeth and arguing with your friends. They've seen you in your real life, and therefore they think they really know you. You're kind of on a pedestal because you're on television, but your pedestal isn't that high. Sharing your intimate details on-screen makes you accessible, and a lot of people feel totally comfortable asking when they can come over to your house and sharing their opinions about your life with you.

After a while, I started to understand that if I was going to go out into the streets of New York I needed to be ready to greet people: "Hello, I'm so happy to see you!" I didn't want to be the type of person who was going to walk by, sunglasses on and head down. I love my fans and want to be accessible to them. That's my whole thing: being accessible, authentic, and relatable.

Along with the people who shouted nice things at me, there were also the people who shouted things that weren't so nice, both in person and on the internet.

"I hate you!"

"You've got a big nose!"

"You're ugly!"

"You're old!"

"You're fat!"

Becoming known as a Housewife was confusing, electrifying, and completely disorienting. I didn't know which way to turn.

I was on *The Real Housewives of New York City* for six seasons. Although I knew most of the girls in my personal life and had been invited to film many times, as I mentioned earlier, I was mainly in the background and therefore not really engaged. I attended the filmed events as an insider, but not as a major participant. There is a perennial wall between the castmates and the people who are invited to be in the background, as I originally was. You can feel that wall and you respect it, which means you avoid getting too close to the camera or approaching the cast too closely. Filming is work. It's also an adrenaline rush. You have to be on your A game while you're being filmed.

With each season, you have to bring something new. You have to peel away the layers and reveal more and more of who you are each year, like an onion. If that is done correctly, the audience will develop a deep relationship with you. They will come to "know you" better with each passing year. And knowing you will include a vast array of emotions. Sometimes they'll love you; sometimes they'll hate you. Sometimes they'll cheer you on and sometimes they'll tear you down. But, at the end of the day, no matter what emotions they're feeling, they will be invested in your role as a Housewife. Here's a metaphor: Housewives are like oysters, spitting out a new pearl each year. Over the years, a necklace is strung together. This is your greater story arc.

When I became a castmate in Season 7, I was already part of the world of the show. I'd known most of the girls for years. One of those girls was Carole Radziwill. Something unexpected happened during my first season of being a castmate. Carole named my house, and this moment was actually caught on-camera. We were in the Berkshires, sitting around the dining table, and Carole was talking about how beautiful the house was and how it wasn't really even a house; it was more like an estate or a manor.

"You should give it a name," she said. Her reasoning was that homes with names tend to be recognized more fully and they also sell better—in case I ever planned on selling.

We continued talking about my great-grandfather and how he used the blue stone that was found on the property to do some of the masonry work. And Carole said, "You should call it Blue Stone Manor."

And that was that. The name was not only fitting but it also had a melodic ring to it. And it was a tribute to my great-grandfather and my grandfather, who'd both worked on its construction.

In Season 7, the audience was introduced to an independent woman who'd been married and divorced and then married and widowed. My reputation after that first year as a castmate was as the sassy fun one who took the audience by storm with her one-liners. People were beginning to warm to me, and nothing too terribly dramatic had happened yet.

For the next five seasons, I continued to get smarter, both on- and off-camera. There are so many idiosyncratic odds and ends that come with being a reality TV star, and unfortunately, nobody gives you a handbook. Through trial and error and by paying attention to what my castmates were doing, I sort of just figured it out.

Off-screen, I got more comfortable doing appearances and I learned how to use social media, which I knew nothing about before *The Housewives*. I started spending more time with old friends who wanted the best for me and less time with people I wasn't sure I trusted. When I went out in public, I was aware that I was a public figure, and so I went out prepared to meet and greet fans.

On-screen, too, I wised up. I showed up for my second season ready to play the game, because now I understood that it *was* a game. I arrived for my first season thinking we were just filming our real lives, and now I understood that, yes, we were filming our real lives—for entertainment. And the best way to entertain is with dramatic action, because ultimately, that's what viewers want to see. The more drama, the better. And I'm not talking about teary-eyed drama either. Sometimes that's fine, but what the audience really wants is excitement.

By the time I started filming for Season 8, I had stronger bonds with both the girls I'd known from before and the girls I'd been introduced to on the show. My new alliances were tested over the course of the season, and a lot of it had to go with my relationship with my then-boyfriend, John, who'd begun to appear more frequently on the show. Some people liked John. Some people didn't.

This—having a romantic relationship scrutinized and examined by first my castmates and then the audience—was totally new to me, and ultimately it forced me to develop a little bit of a thicker skin.

Think about the famous moment in the kitchen of Blue Stone Manor: "I cooked; I decorated; I made it nice!" Since this book is called *Make It Nice* and since the theme behind this statement is at the heart of how I live my life, I'm going to tell you in detail about the events leading up to me saying this line.

In Season 8, I had invited the ladies to Blue Stone Manor for the weekend during Christmastime. I do this every single year, show or not, and every single year, no matter who the guests are, I go above and beyond by planning a wonderful stay for them. I get to the house three or four days early with a team of people to help me transform the space into a winter wonderland. I buy all the food; I pick out the wines and the china; I write out my menus. I assign places at the dinner table for my guests, along with rooms. Each guest gets a candle by their bed and a little welcome gift with their name on it. I create an *atmosphere*, and all I ask of my guests is that they present themselves in a way that's appropriate to the atmosphere.

"You can do whatever you want all day, but at six o'clock at night I want you in my living room for cocktail hour. Then we'll have dinner."

This is what I tell everyone who comes to visit. It's not that hard, right? Just show up at six!

For me, entertaining is a performance art. It's how I express myself. And it's not just the meal. It's the whole thing. I love it. Too much is never enough. I just bought myself a new set of Christian Lacroix china with butterflies on it for Christmas. "Why do we need more china?" Hannah asked, to which I said, "Why *don't* we need it?"

The look of a child when they see Santa Claus is the way I want people to feel when they walk into my house during the holidays. I want to evoke a *feeling*. I want people to *want* to be there, and I want people to talk about it afterwards. I think many of us get so lost on the treadmill of life that we forget to stop and honor tradition. For me, hosting a weekend like this is not only artful, it's also about marking time with big celebrations.

In my mind, getting an invitation is a big deal. You take it seriously. Hello, you've been invited! When I was a kid, Sunday lunches were very important in my house and there was no reason not to show up—unless you were literally dying. If you were sick, you still went to Sunday lunch. If you didn't feel like eating, you still went to Sunday lunch. So, this is all to say that I like an event with a capital *E*. I don't like a loosey-goosey situation. (And that, by the way, is why Brooklyn doesn't work for me.)

My house in the Berkshires is a special place. Just as I honor tradition, I honor my house. It's old. It has history. And I've spent a lot of time perfecting all the small details inside it. If I invite you over to my house, it's a big deal. You should feel honored.

The other tradition within the tradition of Christmastime is that every year, because my birthday is in December, my mother bakes me a traditional homemade vanilla cake with buttercream frosting.

It can't be replicated by anyone else. I look forward to it every year. It's the same cake she's baked for me since I was a little girl, and obviously you know it's very important to me.

So, now you have a sense of how I was feeling before that fateful holiday weekend during Season 8 when my castmates arrived—and immediately got into their squabbles. Luann and Bethenny were at odds about Luann's dating life. Carole was pissed at Luann for calling her a pedophile and then forgetting about it. Everybody ended up in little groups in different rooms talking about one another. So, we were off to a rough start. I was getting increasingly annoyed and feeling totally underappreciated after all the work I'd put into creating a nice weekend.

And then the ladies started making fun of my mom's cake.

Crushed, I got upset. I was unhappy I was being taken for granted. So I shouted several things, culminating with the now-famous, "I cooked; I decorated; I made it nice!"

Of course I didn't know at the time that anybody would care about this sentence. I had no idea that this line would even make it into the show—until six months later, when it spread quickly through the internet. The clip got millions of views in three days. It stunned me. Before I knew it, I was walking down the street and people were shouting at me, "You made it nice!"

This happened in London. And in New York. It happened at the hair salon and in the park. It was happening all the time. I'd be checking out at the grocery store and the cashier would say, "By the way, you made it nice."

And I would say, "I really did! Thank you!"

I think the reason this line had such an impact was that it's so relatable. It was everything that people feel but often don't have the courage to say. When you put a huge amount of effort into something and no one appreciates it, it's a letdown. I think it's very human to want to be acknowledged, and frankly, I don't think women who run households get acknowledged enough for their hard work. Taking care of a home is a real job and doing it well requires a lot of energy.

"Make it nice" has kind of become my trademark saying. It's often used when people introduce me. It's written on the mugs and bags I sell in my online shop. It's the name of my book! At this point, I think they should probably put "Make it nice" on my gravestone.

In Seasons 9, 10, and 11, I really found my stride on the show. I felt more comfortable and like I was truly an integral member of the cast. I'd been officially labeled a Housewife, and I loved it. I felt that it was a badge of honor that, on some level, will live with me forever. No matter what happens for the rest of my life, I will probably always be known as a Housewife. This makes me feel proud because it takes a strong and confident woman to show up honestly and be filmed. The viewers had become more attached to me, and many of them supported me through the good times and the bad. I can't tell you how many times someone on the street has come up to me and told me how they were inspired by something I said on the show, and that to me has been incredibly rewarding.

During these seasons, I doled out some new one-liners, which became known as Dorinda-isms. There was the time I said, "Say it, forget it; write it, regret it" (which is odd, since I'm now writing this book). And there was the time Candace Bushnell asked me how I was doing and I said, "I'll tell you how I'm doing: not well, bitch." Poor Candace was truly in the wrong place at the wrong time. She had no idea what was going on, nor could she have known that she would later become part of an iconic moment on reality television.

Of course, there was also the time, I said, "Clip, clip, clip." I remember this scene vividly.

We had all decided to go to the Bronx and have a girls gangster lunch. Up to this point Sonja and I had been sparring back and forth throughout the season about divorce versus death. Was her divorce as horrible as my widowhood? Strangely, I felt it had not really been taken into account that I had been both divorced *and* widowed by that point.

Anyway, after a date night with John I woke up early to go to the Bronx to film. I was exhausted when I arrived and in a bad mood. Quite frankly, I wanted to cancel, but I felt the right thing to do was show up.

Soon into the lunch, the sparring between Sonja and me started again. I had had enough. So, out of nowhere, I started pinching my fingers and my thumb together, the same gesture you'd make to represent someone talking. "Clip, clip, clip," I said, with my hand talking to Sonja.

As usual, I had no idea this would become a memorable moment on the show. All I was thinking about was how tired I was and how much I wanted to silence Sonja. And then the moment went viral. Like the "I made it nice!" moment, it was relatable. We all know what it's like to want a friend to stop talking, but we often don't say anything because we want to be polite. Well, I said something. And people loved it.

Along with iconic one-liners on the show, there were also the iconic locations. Like the things I said, I never knew what in the background the audience would latch on to. The Fish Room at Blue Stone Manor is a great example. I designed that room in 2007 for my stepson, Aidan, who was twelve at the time. Richard and Aidan loved to go deep-sea fishing together, and when it came time for each child to tell me how they wanted their room decorated, Aidan wanted all of his fish trophies on the wall. Seems innocent enough, correct? Well, the viewers don't know that story. They assumed I'd decorated the house with the show in mind and that Blue Stone Manor was sort of a film set. Obviously, this isn't true. It's my actual home, a home I shared with Richard and three children and decorated accordingly.

This room really got the attention of viewers when Luann said, "I'm not staying in the Fish Room." After that, the room was suddenly called the Fish Room and people were judging my decorative choices. Later, when I finally redecorated the room (because Aidan is a twenty-six-year-old now), the audience assumed I had done that because of what Luann said. People still say this to me now: "Why did you redecorate the Fish Room?!?"

When I look back on the show now, I'm proud of all the moments in which I stood up for myself. I'm proud, too, of when I went to London with Carole to retrieve her late husband's ashes. I talked about Richard then, and Carole and I bonded over the strange circumstances of being relatively young widows and how to find joy in life despite the losses we had endured. There aren't any one-liners from this episode, but there is a lot of heart, and people responded to that. Honesty, whether it's brutal or tender, touches people. People respond to realness.

Watching my moments with Hannah on-screen has made me very proud. I call Hannah my notable citizen. She's smart, witty, honest, and—let's face it—beautiful. Our talks on-camera were the absolute best, and they allowed the viewers to see me as a mother. In the last season, Hannah and I went to Jimmy's, our favorite hamburger joint, and she told me how proud she was of me. I was so moved. I think this moment gave the audience a true glimpse into our relationship. Hannah had watched me suffer, grow, and evolve, and she acknowledged that on-camera for the honest reason that she wanted me to know it. Like the moment with Carole in London, this one was raw, tender, and relatable.

I love, too, the episodes we shot in the Berkshires (or the Berzerkshires, as they were dubbed at some point), because they accurately represent how much I adore my family and decorating for the holidays. I hope that my Christmas spirit brought some joy into people's homes.

In the last season I filmed for *The Housewives* I have some proud moments, and obviously I have some regrets. I definitely wasn't shining my brightest. Still, I didn't expect that it would result in a letting-go.

"You're on pause."

I was shocked. Then I was sad. Then I was humiliated and angry and confused. I was all over the place. I felt left out. Watching the other women go back to work felt like the first year I was out of college. People around me were going back to campus, but I was done.

Sometimes in life, others do for you what you cannot do for yourself, and I now think that's what Bravo did for me. I would never have asked for a break on my own, but maybe I needed a break. Maybe I needed to be pushed out of the nest so I could fly again—and it came right on time. As I told you, every six years I go through a major life transition.

I looked up the definition of "pause." It's an interruption in the action, essentially, and that seems to fit. Now is not a time for more action. It's a time to be still and realign with my greater purpose and have faith that I will emerge as a better version of myself. I've done this before and I'll do it again, and to be honest, I like the new hunger this has ignited in me. Who knows what could happen next? It might be amazing.

It's only by closing a chapter that you are able to see that chapter clearly. Being put "on pause" has given me clarity. I can now see how consuming the show was, for the better and for the worse. The only way to be a Housewife is to be consumed. It's not just a job you do for four months out of the year. It becomes your whole life.

In some ways, being a reality TV personality is like being a professional football player. When you're out on the field, you are playing to win. You can do whatever you want in order to try to win, but as soon as the whistle blows and it's done you pat one another on the ass and you give one another a hand bump and you walk off the field. After you leave, the game is all you talk about. You eat, drink, sleep, and live the game.

This is not a bad thing. It's just the only way to play. You can't dabble in *The Housewives*. You have to be all in. The process takes a lot of effort, both on and off the field. One month of filming is like five months of real life. That's the level of engagement that's required. When you're in it, you forget that you're in it. It just becomes your new normal. Only when you stop can you properly reflect on your experience.

Looking back on these last six years, I can tell you that I have changed. The woman who showed up to that first day of shooting unsure of where the mike was supposed to be attached is not the same woman I am now.

Being a Housewife has been a deeply rewarding process. I grew tremendously. I worked through a lot of my issues on the show, and watching myself on-screen forced me to face them. I learned how to be accountable in the realest sense—because when you're on television everything you say and do is recorded. You can't pretend like it didn't happen. I realized by watching myself that I had some things to work on and that I had some wonderful traits, too. I was proud of how, when faced with conflict, I was able to sort through the facts very quickly and respond succinctly.

The show taught me to be fiercely independent and incredibly aware. I'm more cautious now and more self-protective. Before *The Housewives*, I just kind of assumed people did the right thing and had your best interests at heart. I don't think that now, nor am I expecting anyone to take care of me or defend me. I've learned how to take care of myself. When I was younger I was happy to be in the passenger's seat of my life, and I'm now much happier in the driver's seat, making my own choices.

People are like fire.
You want them to warm you, but not burn you.

Chapter Nine

MAKING IT NICE

A lot has changed in my life, and many times, but my parents have stayed the same. Their house is like a frozen time capsule where I find myself eating like it's 1974 again. This is terrible when you're trying to lose weight, because unlike at a restaurant, I can't say no thanks to the baked potato and the macaroni and the big rolls with butter—and all of this, by the way, is covered in creamy buttermilk dressing. But my mother serves her food with such love that I have to eat it. Even though it's annoying when I'm on a diet, there's really nothing more comforting in the world.

By keeping my roots firmly planted in the reality of where I came from, I can never get too lost. It's also my parents to whom I owe my success. Behind the shiny exterior of the fame I've wandered into are all the years I spent preparing for it, and also all the support I've received, both from my close circle of female friends and from my mom and dad. The reason I start so many phrases with "My mother says . . ." is that my mother's advice has lit the way for me.

Her loving words are what I always come back to when I'm not sure what to do next.

Lately, I've been asking myself, *What is the purpose of having this platform? How can I be useful?*

The answer is that I'd love to light the way for someone, just as my mother has done (and still does!) for me. One of my very favorite things is when a fan comes up to me and says, "I wish you were my mom." What that means to me is that I'm seen as a guide, a voice of reason, a truth teller. I think there are a lot of people out there (and women, I'm especially talking to you) who feel lost and alone. If, by sharing my story and offering some of my wisdom I can help someone, I'd be so glad.

Obviously, nobody wants a preacher. I hate it when people preach to me! I'm not here to tell you what to do. I'm here to offer you advice and to be as honest as I can about it. I'm here to give you options. You can decide how much of my umbrella to use. You can ignore it and get really wet or open it up just a little and get slightly wet. It's up to you, because it's your life.

The only reason anybody is listening to what I have to say is because I try to be authentic, transparent, and tell the truth. The truth hates the dark. I don't believe in hiding. I want to be perfectly imperfect and proud of it. Sometimes I'm loud about how I tell the truth. You don't have to be loud, but do be honest—not only with other people but also with yourself. I've never been a liar, but I spent many years shrinking myself to fit into the lives of other people. Only when Richard died was I given the freedom to fully step into who I am. I know that sounds crass, but guess what? It's true.

Trust is earned when you tell the truth. But the ultimate goal isn't for you to trust me. It's for you to trust yourself. Even though my parents have been hugely supportive all my life, I've learned that some things have to be done alone. I flew the nest and moved into realms that my parents didn't totally understand. They couldn't give me exact advice because they'd never been in the situations I was in. When Richard died, for example, my parents could console me, but they couldn't literally come with me and hold my hand as I went to meet with all those lawyers.

Recently, Hannah gave me a big compliment: "I don't think there's anything that scares you now, Mom."

She said this right after I'd fired a man who had worked for Richard and me for many years. After Richard died, he began to use belittling language, language that I knew would not have been used if Richard had still been alive. I felt like those lawyers had made me feel—like I was being seen as a helpless woman.

My advice to Hannah (and to you) is to get rid of anyone in your life who isn't treating you with respect. And by "get rid of" I mean "good-bye." Don't waste your time trying to change people. It absolutely 100 percent never works.

Hannah's compliment touched my heart, and as far as outside matters are concerned, I think she's right. I know how to handle lawyers and insurance people and all my business affairs. I know how to open my big peacock feathers when necessary to protect myself.

But the truth is, being fearless isn't real. Having fears and taking risks anyway—that's the goal.

It's hard for me to admit my fears, because people count on me. In my family, I'm the one who shows up and gets things done. Hannah counts on me not to fall apart. But, in the spirit of transparency, let me tell you some more about all the fears that keep me up at night.

Since Richard's death, I fear death more poignantly. I used to walk through cemeteries thinking, *Oh, these poor souls died.* Now I think, *Oh, I am going to be one of these poor souls.* I'm aging. My parents are aging. COVID has heightened my fear that they'll die. What would I do without my parents, who've been such rocks for me?

On top of death (a pretty normal fear, I would say), I constantly fear losing everything. This, I know, probably wouldn't be happening if I'd grown up wealthy. The Cinkalas have a terrible fear of (and reverence for) money. A small leak can sink a great ship, as I liked to remind Richard—not that he was listening. But maybe you will be. My fear of waking up tomorrow and being broke feels so real to me sometimes that it's suffocating. Logically, it makes no sense. It would probably take me a while to spend all the money I have. But the feelings—oh wow. They're buried deep in my bones.

What I know, however, is that even if I did lose everything, I would survive. There are so many ways to make money. There are so many concrete actions you can take to survive and make money, and you don't need to be famous or special to do it. Hard work and perseverance pay off.

For anyone who's trying to make money, I would say throw the net out wide, seek out options, and don't be ashamed to promote yourself. Think of yourself as a peacock proudly fanning your feathers! Be open to new opportunities and people. Come from a place of yes and truly mean it. Yes! Say yes to things, because you don't know where opportunities will lead you. At the same time, though, you need to trust your inner voice. Know when to say enough is enough and walk away, because if you don't take care of yourself no one else is going to do it for you. You're responsible for yourself. Take responsibility.

While you're trying to reach your goals, stay healthy physically and mentally so you can make clear decisions. Be mindful of the people you surround yourself with. As my friend Greg's mother always says, "Show me your friends and I'll tell you who you are." Something that's been superhelpful for me is to never ask, *Why me?* A much better question is, *Why not me?* You don't need to be a victim of circumstance. You are in charge of your life.

If you mess up, it's fine. My mom always says, "Life is like a quilt filled with many patches, some more beautiful than others, and that's what makes up the quilt: all of it." Don't be afraid of embarrassment, because honestly, who cares what other people think? Be the person you want to see in the mirror. At the end of the day, you answer to yourself and your family and no one else.

You're the only one of you out there, so lean into who you are. If you're like, *But who am I?* that's okay. Get a role model. I love Iris Apfel. She's a businesswoman, an interior decorator, an influencer, a fashion icon, and, so important, she was a wife for sixty-seven years to her husband, Carl. She's ninety-nine years old, colorful and unique with her trademark glasses and style choices. I don't think Iris Apfel cares what anybody thinks. She has consistently been a trailblazer for women and creatives, wacky and wonderful, and personally, she's taught me to go for it in life and do what you love. Be you and people can take it or leave it. My favorite quote of hers is "I don't see anything wrong with a wrinkle. It's kind of a badge of courage." I *agree*!

To me, becoming a successful person isn't only about external achievements. When I sit next to somebody at a dinner and they tell me about their résumé, I'm not impressed. What I want to know is how the person got to where they are today. What obstacles have they overcome? How many times have they gotten their heart broken? How many deaths have they been close to? That stuff, to me, is what's interesting, because the obstacles are what shape us and make us strong. If you tell me you went to Ivy League schools and got all the right jobs, I'm just not that interested in you, sorry. I'm not saying that you have to go through hard times to be interesting. I'm just saying, don't lead with your external achievements. It's not what I want to know. You're allowed to be a real person and talk about what is actually going on with you. If you're trying too hard to impress, it does the opposite of what you want. It's unimpressive.

During the dark times in my life when I have felt alone and overwhelmed by fear, my mother has reminded me that the answer is not to lie in bed trying to solve the riddle of my life. The answer is to just start. "Get out of bed. Wash your face. Take a walk." These small and simple instructions have gotten me through some of the bleakest periods. I would get out of bed and wash my face and take a walk, and before I knew it I was feeling better again.

The truth is that it's easy to get stuck in life. Getting overwhelmed is normal. If you're in the thick of it right now, I'm here to remind you to just start. Take one small action, then another, then another, and pretty soon you'll find that you are moving forward again. If you have a friend who's stuck, you might consider calling to check in on them. We all feel so alone sometimes, and little kindnesses can really make a difference in people's lives.

If you're in a dark place, the other thing I would add, along with the advice to just start somewhere, is not to add to your darkness with more darkness. After Richard died, I drank angrily. I drank to self-medicate, as I mentioned. I drank to forget. And it put me into a worse place. I wasn't a good mother during that period. I was depressed. If I'm happy and drinking, it's a different story. I go out and have a few with friends, and I wake up content. So, I've learned that for me, I have to stay away from alcohol when I'm feeling confused or fearful. Alcohol is, after all, a depressant. I don't know what your particular brand of darkness is, but stay away from alcohol when you're feeling sad. You want to be going up, not down.

When I look back on my life, I can see that everything is as it should have been, even the bad stuff. Every moment was a stepping-stone to the next moment. When something happens in your life that seems insurmountable, it's not. It's always surmountable. After you get to the other side, you'll see that. Every time I have gone through pain, I have grown. Every heartache has added a new and interesting layer to who I am.

People like to say that life is full of twists and turns. Well, I actually think it's full of roadblocks and stop signs, and it's up to you to manage your next move. If you're going to accept the roadblocks and stop signs and not look for a way around them, then those are choices.

As my mother likes to say, "In life there are people who never climb over the mountain. They just stay where they are. There are other people who climb a little bit and then set up camp there. The air is quite nice at that higher altitude. It's not too thin yet. It's not too difficult. So they stay there on the side of the mountain. And then there are the true hikers. They trudge right up into the clouds, where the air is so thin that it's scary. Those are the people who are willing to venture into the unknown."

Every time I've ventured into the unknown, it's been absolutely horrible in the moment, because struggling is hard! Every single time, I have thought, *My life is ending*. When Richard died, I thought my life was over. When I spent my Liz Claiborne bonus on drinks for everyone at the bar and had to move back home with no money and my tail between my legs, I thought I was a failure. Only later was I able to see that going broke made me more careful with money, and only later was I able to understand how Richard's death gave me a new outlook on life.

Every situation that has seemed negative at the time has actually turned out to be positive. All my hardest moments have deepened my capacity for love and led me to double down on myself, because whenever I climbed over another mountain it reinforced the truth that I was strong.

So, if you think your life is ending because you messed up, it's probably not. You're probably just learning something new. Now is the time to be still and let things unfold organically. If you get confused about this, pay attention to nature. Recently, I was looking at my rhododendrons, thinking they were done for the season, because it had started to get cold. Then—bam—they had a last burst of growth. An abundance of tiny vibrant buds appeared. It reminded me of what I've learned so many times. There is always life after life—and it often appears unexpectedly.

I think it's very important to have specific goals. Decide where you want to end up and then point yourself in that direction and start walking. The funny thing, though, is that you're never going to get to where you want to go in the exact way you expected. The journey is going to be a zigzag trail, not a straight line. No matter what, don't give up. And don't waste your time trying to predict the future either. You have to handle each situation as it comes. If you need to rest, then rest. I love naps; I take one every afternoon! When you're done resting, get up and keep going. Just keep going. If you don't believe in yourself, then pretend like you do. Fake it till you make it. Eventually, your faking will become a reality. As you keep moving through your struggles, you'll come to believe in yourself.

Life is about learning. Everybody has something to teach you, as Richard used to say—and that means everybody. The cashier at the store, the college professor, and the woman you dislike all have wisdom to offer. I think a lot of people incorrectly assume that only certain experiences, like ones that end in pain or loss, have something to teach us, but that's not true. Every single person and every single bit of life is a learning moment if you're paying attention. What does that mean? That you have to pay attention. Listen. Be open. Don't close yourself off to opportunities you might think are beneath you, because you never know where things will lead. The smallest, crappiest job could end up leading you to your biggest success.

I learn about life in the same way I learned how to cook from my mother. I watch and I listen. Taking diligent notes and writing out a recipe for your perfect life is fine, but there's a distancing in that. The real way to learn is by feeling the experience emotionally. I couldn't tell you how long, exactly, to cook my mother's lasagna, but I could show you how the cheese is supposed to look when it's done. Anybody can read self-help books, but it's participating in your life that teaches the true lessons. It's like reading about a painting. That might be nice for some reasons, but eventually, don't you want to just go look at the painting?

For a lot of my life, I thought of myself as the underdog. In elementary school, I was the kid who protected the kids who were being bullied. I hate injustice. I've been the whistle-blower, the one who calls it like she sees it. In the story of David and Goliath, I'd always considered myself David. He's the underdog.

Well, Hannah recently told me that I'm not David. I'm Goliath. I appear to be a strong warrior, but in the end, I'm quite fragile and can be taken down. "You're not the underdog, Mom. You're the fallible warrior." Maybe Hannah's right. I spent a lot of my younger years thinking I had something to prove. It took me a while to realize that I don't have anything to prove. I'm worthy just as I am.

In going over my life story for this book, I've done a lot of thinking about what I would tell my younger self. If I could go back and talk to her, I'd say, "You're worthy, Dorinda! You don't have to earn your seat at the table. You already have a seat at the table."

Looking back, I wish that I had put myself first more often. I wish I'd been a little greedier and more selfish and able to articulate my needs more efficiently. I had a tendency, as a young person, to get lost in the shuffle. When anything went wrong—*My life is over!*—I panicked. And in my panic, I can see now that I didn't always make the best decisions. Maybe I climbed the mountain too fast sometimes, and the air at the top was so thin that it scared me. When I got bogged down by fear, I made things harder than they needed to be. I've learned more patience now. When life gets tough, sometimes the best thing to do is stop and take a breath.

I would also say to my younger self, "Good job!" Because no matter what was happening in my life, I was doing my best. I've always tried very hard. I've taken risks even when I was full of fear. I've also tried a lot of different things. I've worked in fashion and in real estate and signed up to be a reality TV star. I've been fluid about my career identity and my personal identity. I've been married; I've been divorced; I've been single; I've been widowed. I'm proud of how I've followed the natural zigzagging flow to arrive at all these different identities and how I haven't clung to any of them too hard. All the chapters of my life have been wonderfully colorful in their own ways, and each chapter, I can see now, served an important purpose.

While I've lived in many places and worn many hats, so to speak, at my core I haven't changed. Maybe I've deepened, but fundamentally, I've always relied on the same foundation of family, spirituality, and humor. That's the other thing I would advise you to do on your journey: laugh! Life is so crazy sometimes that what else can you do but joke about it?

The best thing about being older is that I've checked all the major boxes. Childhood, check. Marriage, check. Motherhood, check. Financial security, check! The next boxes I want to check are about internal rather than external things. They're about finding joy. The great gift of being put on pause is that now I'm not only looking at the next season of the *Housewives*, I'm also considering the next season of my life. What does that look like?

I have a strong feeling that my next phase is going to be my best yet, because what I have now is absolute freedom. I can do as much or as little as I want—and I can make it all about me. I'm not responsible for anyone; I don't have a job or a husband; I never have to marry again if I don't want to. Instead of boxes I feel obligated to check, I have an ocean of possibilities. I could move to the Bahamas if I felt like it, or devote myself to a new cause, or learn to paint the landscape around Blue Stone Manor.

I don't know what the details of my future will entail, because what am I? A fortune-teller? What I do know is that I want to keep learning and growing. I want to stay healthy. Since COVID began, I've started playing the piano again, which I hadn't done since college after years of my mother insisting I know how to play an instrument and sending me to lessons as a girl. I'm knitting. And, of course, I've also been decorating and cooking up a storm. In short, I'm doing all the things that make me happy and relaxed.

Connecting to fans is one of my absolute favorite parts of my current life. I love receiving emails from fans, and I respond to every one of them. I feel that if somebody puts in the effort to write to you about their life, then the human thing to do is respond.

Recently, a young woman from Canada wrote to me. She told me that she'd suffered through a difficult upbringing and then in her teen years had met the love of her life—who was also a drug user. Seven years into their relationship, he died of an overdose. She thanked me for being honest on the show about my grieving Richard's death. I am so honored and touched when I receive messages like these. Here's what I wrote back to her:

Thank you so much for reaching out and sharing your story with me. I am so sorry to hear about your difficult journey and your boyfriend's passing. Life, at the end of the day, just isn't fair. With that said, I would ask you to look at this time as an ending to one part of your journey and the beginning of another.

Life is filled with stop signs and roadblocks. This is not the time to give up. It's time to move around the obstacles. As unfortunate as it is, your boyfriend seems to have made some not-so-good choices that not only contributed to his passing but maybe, just maybe, would have negatively affected you long-term, so try to use this time as a learning curve.

Please use this time to think, pray, and go forward. Cry when you need to, and remember to love and cherish. No matter what, get up each day and try to put one foot in front of the other. Life can and will move forward again, but it is up to you to be strong and go forth. Grief is necessary, but it shouldn't stop your life.

I hope this helps and I also hope you use this terrible time to learn and move ahead with the knowledge that anything is possible and that pain and loss can be valuable tools to make a better life.

Sending you a hug from Blue Stone Manor. I am so sorry for your loss.

For all of you who are going through hard times, I'd say the same thing I said to this woman. Just keep going. Making it nice doesn't only mean presenting a beautiful façade. It's not only about decorating and cooking. It's about all the work you put into it. It's about all the obstacles you overcome to get to the part that is beautiful.

Remember, success isn't measured by your achievements. It's measured by how you handle the ups and downs of life. As you go forward on your path, keep your head up. Do what you believe in.

Tell the truth, be transparent, stay strong, learn from your mistakes, and keep trying no matter what.

Well, I guess it's good-bye for now. I hope you have enjoyed reading this book. I hope it has helped you to know me a little better and I hope that you can take away a few good lessons on life, love, work, family, and "making it nice"!

xxxx

Dorinda

ACKNOWLEDGMENTS

I am so happy that I am able to share this book about my journey with you. I hope first and foremost that you've enjoyed it, and that it has made you laugh, cry, think, and learn. There's no right or wrong in life, and there's no straight path. Life requires the willingness to put yourself out there, try your best, and accept yourself, warts and all.

So I mean it when I say: Life is a quilt of colorful patches—some more beautiful than others, but in the end, collectively amazing.

I want to thank my Italian and Polish grandparents. Their love and guidance is still with me today.

Thank you to my mother, who is my queen. The invisible string of love that binds you, me, and Hannah is eternal.

To my father, my rock. You are the standard of what a father and husband should be. I love you so much, and I am so grateful.

To my Hannah, my daughter, my love, my heartbeat, and my greatest achievement. Best editor ever!

To my brothers and sister, John, Dean, and Melinda: Thank you for always being there in the good times and bad.

To Ralph, Hannah's dad, for being an outstanding father, and standing by me even after we divorced.

And finally to my love, Richard, my husband: As you said to me on our wedding day, you are my north. You are no longer with me physically, but I feel your love, protection, and guidance every day. Our time together was short, but our love and commitment were fierce and undying. (I bet you can't believe I wrote a book! Yes, Richard, I wrote a whole book.)

Thank you to the beautiful extended family of friends I've had the honor of having in my life over the years. We have shared laughter and tears together, and I appreciate each and every one of you.

To Len, who has been by my side for sixteen years.

To NBCUniversal, Bravo, and Shed Productions, for giving me an incredible experience and platform.

To Natasha Simons, my editor at Simon & Schuster, Maggie Loughran, associate editor, and everyone at Gallery Books: Thank you for believing in me and pushing me to write this book.

To Connor Goldsmith, my literary agent: It was a long road, but we got there in the end!

To Swan: Thank you for turning endless stories and experiences into organized chapters.

In life, you need to stop dreaming and start doing. Little by little, you'll achieve your dream—and have many stories to tell in the end.